LITERARY MISCELLANY

EVERYTHING YOU ALWAYS WANTED TO KNOW ABOUT LITERATURE

LITERARY MISCELLANY

EVERYTHING YOU ALWAYS WANTED TO KNOW ABOUT LITERATURE

ALEX PALMER

Skyhorse Publishing

Skyhorse Publishing books may be purchased in bulk at special discounts for sales promotion, corporate gifts, fund-raising, or educational purposes. Special editions can also be created to specifications. For details, contact the Special Sales Department, Skyhorse Publishing, 555 Eighth Avenue, Suite 903, New York, NY 10018 or info@skyhorsepublishing.com.

www.skyhorsepublishing.com

10 9 8 7 6 5 4 3 2 1

Library of Congress Cataloging-in-Publication Data

Palmer, Alex, 1981-
   Literary miscellany : everything you always wanted to know about literature / Alex Palmer.
       p. cm.
   Includes bibliographical references.
   ISBN 978-1-61608-095-2 (hardcover : alk. paper)
   1. Literature--Miscellanea. 2. Literary curiosa. I. Title.
   PN43.P36 2010
   802--dc22
                                        2010027205

Printed in China

They are the books, the arts, the academes,
That show, contain, and nourish all the world.
—William Shakespeare, *Love's Labour's Lost*

CONTENTS

Part - II: Readers

Why audiences love, hate, or ignore the great works of literature

ACKNOWLEDGMENTS

I am grateful to Ann Treistman and Skyhorse Publishing, without whom this book would not exist, as well as my wonderful friends and family, whose support and suggestions made this a much better book than it otherwise would have been. Special thanks to Nick for all his input and to Jenn for her patience and general wonderfulness.

INTRODUCTION

The writing of this book began with some simple questions: Who was the first literary villain? What's the difference between a novella and a novel? These soon led to other, often more complicated, questions. I tackle some big topics here, from the rocky beginnings of the novel to the history of children's literature, but every chapter ultimately comes down to the same question for the reader: Why should I care? It's my hope that you'll find an answer to this question on every page (or at least every few pages).

This book looks at diverting aspects of the great works and authors, while also offering plenty of facts that you've always wanted to know about literature, or perhaps have never considered. Who knew that satire, from *Gulliver's Travels* to *The Daily Show*, can be traced back to two ancient Romans who mastered the art of insulting people—one who was pretty nice, one who was a certifiable jerk? Or that some of literature's greatest authors have perpetrated some seriously shocking (and often hilarious) hoaxes?

I hope this book helps remind you just how much fun books can be—perhaps even entertaining enough to compete with reality TV shows and Facebook. Many epic poems and dense novels have just as much sex, drugs, and violence (and, of course, relevant, thought-provoking ruminations) to keep even the shortest attention span riveted.

Literary Miscellany makes no claim to be comprehensive. Some major writers and works get less attention here than one would probably expect, and others more: As a pioneer of detective fiction, short stories, and alcohol abuse, Edgar Allan Poe pops up frequently in these pages, while a giant like James Joyce is only occasionally mentioned. Popular fiction writers like J. K. Rowling and Stephen King get slightly more ink than masters like John Dryden and Alfred, Lord Tennyson. Although we can't cover everything in these few pages, I expect you will find each chapter an entertaining and informative read.

GREAT OPENERS

"The sun shone, having no alternative, on the nothing new."

—*Murphy* by Samuel Beckett

"The sky above the port was the color of television, tuned to a dead channel."

—*Neuromancer* by William Gibson

"A screaming comes across the sky."

—*Gravity's Rainbow* by Thomas Pynchon

"Whether I shall turn out to be the hero of my own life, or whether that station will be held by anybody else, these pages must show."

—*David Copperfield* by Charles Dickens

"If you really want to hear about it, the first thing you'll probably want to know is where I was born, and what my lousy childhood was like, and how my parents were occupied and all before they had me, and all that *David Copperfield* kind of crap, but I don't feel like going into it, if you want to know the truth."

—*The Catcher in the Rye* by J. D. Salinger

"I am an American, Chicago born—Chicago, that somber city—and go at things as I have taught myself, free-style, and will make the record in my own way: first to knock, first admitted; sometimes an innocent knock, sometimes a not so innocent."

—*The Adventures of Augie March* by Saul Bellow

"Call me Ishmael."

—*Moby-Dick* by Herman Melville

PART I

WRITERS

*The lives, habits, and
bizarre personalities of the greats*

WHAT DO HOMER AND JAY-Z HAVE IN COMMON?

Bards and epic storytelling

Before novelists, publishers, or Amazon.com existed, bards, or oral poets, ruled the literary scene. So this seems like the right topic to begin with. Proliferating through medieval Europe, and Britain in particular, until around the seventeenth century, these poets were multitaskers, composing and memorizing stories and reciting them for their audience, often while playing a harp, lyre, or some other ancient instrument.

Their tales celebrated the deeds of great men, catalogued the genealogies of kings and princes, and relayed the exciting historical events and victories of the tribe down through the generations. They preceded the rhapsodes and king's poets of later generations, but also share some striking similarities with another type of performer prevalent today: rappers and hip-hop stars.

Bards were boosters. Like a rapper giving love to his music label or mentor, a bard would weave in positive stories about the wealthy royals who sponsored him and offer eulogies and tales of glory about his employers' ancestors. Since it was almost entirely an oral culture, it was up to the bards to remember the key details of past glories and family history and to pass these on to the rest of their tribe—so the leaders of the day made sure to take care of their poets.

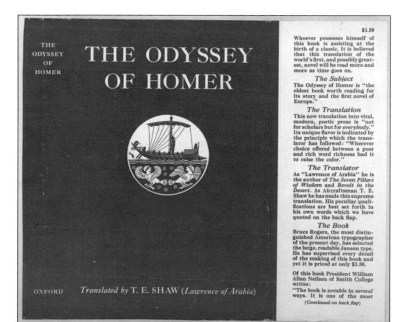

Terms for the oral poets varied by region, with different class designations for each. In Ireland, bards ranked below the class of poets known as *fili*. To become a *fili* required more formal learning. A *fili* could move up the ranks as he learned more stories and improved his skill, the highest level being the *ollam*, who could recite 350 stories, which took some twelve years to learn:

1. *ollam*—350 stories	6. *macfuirmid*—40 stories
2. *drnuth*—175 stories	7. *fochlocon*—30 stories
3. *clí*—80 stories	8. *drisoc*—20 stories
4. *cano*—60 stories	9. *toman*—10 stories
5. *doss*—50 stories	10. *oblaire*—7 stories

In Wales, bards shared similarities with the Irish *fili*—receiving the level of respect that a smith, cleric, or other highly trained professional earned. The Welsh had just three levels of bards, the highest of which was *pencerdd* ("master-poet" or "chief of song"). To avoid getting too technical, in this chapter the term "bard" will encompass all these terms.

Once they graduated from this learning, the poets would travel from house to house and village to village, getting VIP treatment from those they dropped in on. The poets traveled with an entourage of assistants and lower bards (the Welsh sometimes dubbed these lower bards *bardd teulu*, or "bard of the bodyguard").

As with rappers, bards proved their skills by competing with each other, sometimes in highly publicized events. The national Eisteddfod, an annual festival that began in Wales as far back as 1176, developed into the biggest of such events. Over a period of several days, bards performed their songs and poems before judges. The one chosen as the winner received a carved oak chair, which he used to tell stories and instruct young poets.

This served as both a test for young bards and a proving ground for the already established poets. The Eisteddfod was discontinued in the late seventeenth century, but then revived a century later. The annual National Eisteddfod is still a huge cultural event for Wales; more than 6,000 poets competed in the 2006 summit, which welcomed 150,000 visitors—more fans than a typical Jay-Z concert can boast!

Did You Know?

John Dryden once famously played host to his own poetry competition. He and a group of wits, including the earls of Dorset and Buckingham, decided to each write a selection, with Dryden selecting the best one. After reviewing most of them, he got to the Earl of Dorset's and immediately awarded him the prize. His poem? "I promise to pay John Dryden, / or order on demand, / the sum of 500 pounds."

Villagers treated a bard well when he went on tour, because someone who disagreed with a poet (or with his employer) could wind up in one of the poet's derisive satires. If a host acted rudely, or a patron neglected to pay what he had promised, the poet called him out in a *glam dicin*, ensuring a rotten reputation as a cheapskate or worse. Some believed that a really pointed satire caused boils to appear on the target's face.

Despite—or perhaps because of—this fear, not everyone loved the bards. When Edward I conquered Wales in 1277, he supposedly sent hundreds of the poets to their deaths in an attempt to keep them from inciting rebellion and retelling a version of history he would rather not hear.

How did epic storytellers remember all those lines?

A bard earned respect for his ability to remember lengthy stories full of historic details as much as how well he told his tales. So how did he remember all that? Historians believe bards learned formulas of specific meter and alliterative rhyme, which gave their works a consistent, memorable flow. This explains the regular, repeated phrasing and episodic structure of epics like *The Iliad* and *Beowulf.* Like lyric-heavy rap songs with catchy hooks, these formulas allowed them to transition easily from one part to the next, making their storytelling smooth and casual.

We don't know much about any bards, but Homer may be the most mysterious of them all. While it is widely agreed that he lived in the eighth century BC in Ionia (what is now considered Turkey), that is about all that is agreed on. It is unclear that *The Iliad* and *Odyssey* were written by the same person, as they are significantly different tales, though there is not enough evidence to disprove this, either.

Because he delivered his work orally, Homer almost certainly borrowed (or perhaps sampled) ideas and anecdotes from his contemporaries. However, he imbued his epics with his unique sense of narrative and tone, just as a musician might remix elements of other songs. As critic Daniel S. Burt explains in *The*

Literary 100, "To achieve the dramatic unity and coherence of his epics . . . is almost unthinkable and a testimony to Homer's unmatched skill as a poet and storyteller."

Did You Know?

The novelist Samuel Butler studied Homer extensively and, after considering the historical and geographical information in the poem, as well as the poet's particular techniques, determined Homer must have been "a very young woman" living in Sicily. He published *The Authoress of the Odyssey*, outlining this theory, in 1897.

The extensive literary and cultural traditions built around oral poetry helped ensure its longevity, and it thrived from generation to generation for centuries. After the French-speaking Normans conquered England in 1066 and eventually took control of Ireland and Wales, the poets were incorporated into the court as entertainers and genealogists. The Gaelic culture waned, and the duties of the bards shifted to involve written literature; their function evolved into the roles of court poet and troubadour, with the more familiar patron/artist relationship becoming the standard (see next chapter). By the mid-seventeenth century, the role of oral poets, with their emphasis on the social function of their work, had largely been ceded to the individualism and private enterprise of the new class of poets.

Calling All Poets

The term "bard" has also come to mean any serious poet, the best-known example being William Shakespeare, also known as "The Bard of Avon." Many other poets have been dubbed with much snappier titles. These include:

The Blind Bard

Homer (c. 750 BC) was called "The Blind Bard," but there is little actual evidence that he was blind. Some believe the character of the blind poet Demodocus in the *Odyssey* is meant to represent the work's author himself.

The Bard of Democracy

Walt Whitman, who wrote *The Democratic Review* (1841–1845) and *Democratic Vistas* (1871).

The Bard of Hope

Thomas Campbell, the author of *The Pleasures of Hope* (1799).

The Bard of the Imagination

Mark Akenside, author of *The Pleasures of the Imagination* (1744), a long didactic poem about the enjoyment of beauty, philosophy, and the study of man.

HOW DID STARVING WRITERS PAY THE BILLS?

The patrons, odd jobs, and odder merchandising of the masters

William Somerset Maugham once said, "Money is like a sixth sense—and you can't make use of the other five without it." Making a living as a writer has never been easy, and throughout the history of literature, authors and poets have engaged in some surprising, and sometimes embarrassing, gigs to keep food on the table as they pursued their passion.

For centuries, writers did not have the option of making a living solely from writing. From the fourteenth to the seventeenth centuries, writers, such as bards and kings' poets, focused their energies on finding patrons who would support their work, developing a two-way relationship: the patron paid the writer's way, while a great writer helped boost the aristocrat's prestige or political strength. Since power and glory could be fleeting things, members of the court saw immortalization in a poem as a valuable thing worth a decent amount of cash. The job was not all courtly poetry and grand odes; working for a patron could often involve writing inscriptions and histories or serving as a tutor or diplomat when the occasion required.

Did You Know?

Legend has it that when Edmund Spenser failed to receive payment from his patron, he sent a piece of paper to Queen Elizabeth reading, "I was promised on a time, / To have reason for my rhyme; / From that time unto this season, / I received nor rhyme nor reason."

The writer and his patron had an intricate relationship, with the writer's work influenced by his employer's tastes. The classical relationship between Virgil and his patron, Maecenas, was held as the ideal, based on an ancient epigram that translates, "Let there be Maecenases . . . and Virgils will not be lacking." Some notable "Maecenases" include:

- Robert Dudley, Earl of Leicester—A close friend of Queen Elizabeth's, Dudley was patron to poets including Philip Sidney (his nephew) and Edmund Spenser.
- Henry Wriothesley, Earl of Southampton—Shakespeare's patron, to whom the poet dedicated *Venus and Adonis* (1593) and *The Rape of Lucrece* (1594). He is thought to be the "Mr. W. H." to whom Shakespeare's sonnets are addressed, disguised through a reversal of his initials.
- Elizabeth Sidney—Daughter of Philip and a patron to Ben Jonson, who wrote "To Penhurst" in honor of her family.
- Francis Walsingham—Patron to both Francis Bacon and Christopher Marlowe. He was also Queen Elizabeth's "spymaster," who likely employed Marlowe as an agent (and some believe ordered the poet's assassination).

As patronage faded with the Renaissance, a publishing industry aimed at a broader readership began to grow. The copyright act of 1709 was the first to recognize the legal right of authorship, although it would be decades before the notion of copyright was seen as originating with the author. The act did free the publisher from the monopoly of the printer, allowing the industry to expand in both Britain and the United States.

Paradise Sold

Milton signed an agreement with Samuel Simmons in April 1667, giving the bookseller copyright of *Paradise Lost* for five pounds (plus five pounds for three subsequent editions) earning him a whopping ten pounds for the greatest epic in English. Adding insult to injury, his widow sold all remaining rights to Simmons for eight pounds.

Daniel Defoe is considered the first person to actually make a living as a working writer. The success of *Robinson Crusoe* (1719) came at a time when the technology of printing and rising rate of literacy among the English meant that enough books were being produced and sold to afford a reasonable payment to the author (though they remained prohibitively expensive for the average Brit). It was only the occasional mega-selling author who could afford to live on writing alone.

As publishing houses established themselves by the late eighteenth century, a system of royalties allowed authors to compose works more freely, targeted to the demands of the expanding market. The establishment of circulation libraries and

strengthening copyright laws helped publishing to become profitable enough that by 1776, Samuel Johnson could proclaim "No man but a blockhead ever wrote, except for money."

By the beginning of the nineteenth century, authors

The Secret of Success

Chapter One

could make a living writing articles and books, but piracy remained rampant, particularly in America, and a writer could easily be ripped off if he wasn't careful. Edgar Allan Poe received nine dollars to publish "The Raven" in the *Evening Mirror* in 1845. Readers loved it, but when many other publishers printed their own version of the poem, few bought Poe's official collection when he published it months later.

Other writers knew their business better. Charles Dickens is credited with pioneering the serialized novel, as well as republishing popular works into "special editions." Going on lecture tours also provided moneymaking opportunities to nineteenth-century writers.

Merchandising Mark

Mark Twain may have said, "a banker is a person who lends you his umbrella when the sun is shining and wants it back the minute it rains," but he knew a thing or two about finding sources for cash. Besides his books, which sold quite well, Twain put his trademark to all types of products, and a few misguided inventions. These include:

- Mark Twain's Memory Builder board game (one critic described it as "a cross between an income tax form and a table of logarithms")
- Mark Twain Cigars, featuring the slogan "Known to Everyone and Liked by All," as well as Mark Twain Tobacco
- Twain printing machine
- Self-pasting scrapbook (one of his bestsellers, eventually selling some 25,000 units)
- Whiskey
- The Twain Bed Clamp (designed to keep babies from getting caught under the covers).

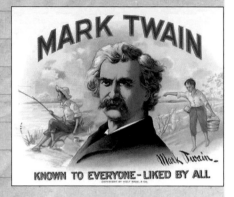

As writing became more profitable, some authors even embraced the craft as just another job. Jack London, the first writer to make a million dollars from writing, generally saw his work as a business more than an artistic enterprise. He said, "I write a book for no other reason than to add three or four hundred acres to my magnificent estate."

The evolution of publishing and book marketing through the twentieth century allowed successful authors to bring in good money in royalties, as well as through optioning their works for film or television adaptations. Before they gained literary prestige, authors worked a number of fascinating day jobs.

Kurt Vonnegut managed America's first Saab dealership in Cape Cod during the late 1950s. He joked in a 2004 essay, "I now believe my failure as a dealer so long ago explains what would otherwise remain a deep mystery: Why the Swedes have never given me a Nobel Prize for Literature." Richard Wright worked as a letter sorter in a post office on the South Side of Chicago from 1927 to 1930, while he wrote a number of short stories and poems that were published in literary journals.

William Faulkner also worked in the postal service, as postmaster at the University of Mississippi, before his writing career took off. He neatly summarized the balance of art and commerce faced by many authors in his resignation note from that gig: "As long as I live under the capitalist system I expect to have my life influenced by the demands of moneyed people. But I will be damned if I propose to be at the beck and call of every itinerant scoundrel who has two cents to invest in a postage stamp. This, sir, is my resignation."

In some cases, a writer's day job could help jump-start his or her writing career. Toni Morrison was a successful editor at Random House for several years before publishing her first novel. Even after her writing took off, she continued working there, discovering such writers as Chinua Achebe, Toni Cade Bambara, and Gayl Jones.

A more fortuitous example of a writer working the right job at the right time came as a busboy interrupted the poet Vachel Lindsay as he dined at a hotel restaurant in Washington, D.C. At first irritated by the young man, who handed him some sheets of his poetry, Lindsay was quickly impressed by the writing and asked the busboy, "Who wrote this?" The busboy replied, "I did," and so Langston Hughes got his first big break.

At Least It Made Top 100

On CareerCast.com's 2010 survey of the 100 best and worst jobs, book author placed number 74. Not bad, although it ranked below forklift operator (#67) and musical instrument repairer (#62).

This list of some other day jobs of the greats gives one a sense of what these authors might have done if they hadn't made it as writers:

- T. S. Eliot worked as a banker—specifically serving as a clerk for Lloyds Bank of London for eight years, during which time he found inspiration for *The Waste Land* while walking to work.
- J. D. Salinger served as entertainment director on the MS *Kungsholm,* a Swedish luxury liner. These experiences informed his short story "Teddy," which takes place on a liner.
- William S. Burroughs worked as an exterminator.
- Douglas Adams worked as a hotel security guard in London.
- Franz Kafka worked as chief legal secretary of the workmen's accident insurance institute and is believed by at least one professor to have invented the hard hat during this time.

More recently, financial fortune has ironically become something of an embarrassment to successful authors. In *The Fight* (1975), Norman Mailer describes receiving a million-dollar advance for his novel. In his signature third-person style, Mailer writes how, "He knew that his much publicized novel (still nine-tenths to be written) would now have to be twice as good as before to overcome such financial news. Good literary men were not supposed to pick up *sums.*"

The £500,000 Martin Amis received for his 1995 book *The Information* earned such publicity and criticism that his publisher HarperCollins released the book two months ahead of schedule to take advantage of the attention. Novelist A. S. Byatt described

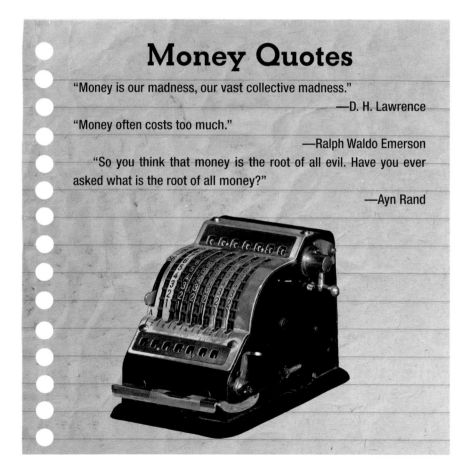

Money Quotes

"Money is our madness, our vast collective madness."

—D. H. Lawrence

"Money often costs too much."

—Ralph Waldo Emerson

"So you think that money is the root of all evil. Have you ever asked what is the root of all money?"

—Ayn Rand

the episode as "extremely bad for the industry," saying that it "makes life hard for young authors." Even in success, writing can be thankless work.

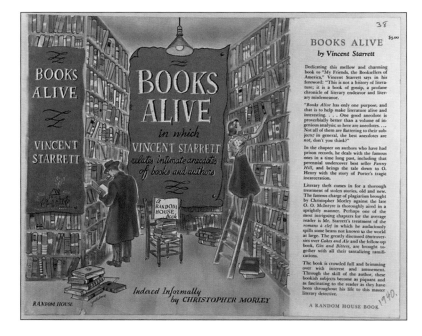

IS COFFEE OR OPIUM BETTER FOR CREATIVITY?

Writers and their rotten habits

In Canto II of *The Inferno*, Dante Alighieri calls out, "O Muses, O high genius, aid me now!" While this practice of invoking a muse for inspiration fell out of popularity with epic poetry, writers have continued to reach for plenty of other, less divine, "aids" to help them tap their creative energies. Whether it is Jack Kerouac slipping Benzedrine into his coffee to help him power through a marathon writing session, or Edgar Allan Poe hitting the bottle to take him to the dark place of his tales, drugs have been not-so-trusty sidekicks to many authors seeking all manner of inspiration.

While Homer and Shakespeare made occasional references to various potions, it was Thomas de Quincey's *Confessions of an English Opium-Eater* (1821) that really lit up literature's experimentation with drugs. De Quincey's autobiographical account of the pleasures and pains of opium use aroused the interest of the Romantics, especially considering the drug's tendency to produce vivid dreams and help artists access places that the sober mind would not go. Lord Byron, Samuel Taylor Coleridge, and Percy Bysshe Shelley were all regular users (virtually all of the Romantics dabbled in it, excluding William Wordsworth).

Coleridge's "Kubla Khan" credits its surreal images to an opium-induced "Vision in a Dream" that was cruelly interrupted by a visitor waking the poet up and seriously bumming his high. Coleridge's opium addiction caused him plenty of trouble later in life, as he separated from his wife, became estranged from his lifelong friend Wordsworth, and had himself put under the care of a doctor until his death.

Did You Know?

Byron had less trouble with opium than he did with laxatives. Historians believe he suffered from severe anorexia nervosa, including starvation diets during which he would survive only on biscuits and water, as well as the regular use of strong laxatives that kept him far below a healthy weight.

Opium's popularity in the nineteenth century, often mixed with alcohol in the form of laudanum, related to the fact that it was prescribed as a painkiller for everything from headaches to tuberculosis. Louisa May Alcott got hooked after taking it for typhoid fever. Coleridge first took it for rheumatism. Elizabeth Barrett Browning began using it at fifteen years old for spinal tuberculosis and soon argued that it greatly enhanced her imagistic poetry, writing to her brother in 1843 that, "I am in a fit of writing—could write all day & night—& long to live by myself for 3 months in a forest of chestnuts and cedars, in an hourly succession of poetical paragraphs and morphine draughts."

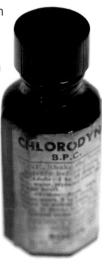

Did You Know?

A combination of laudanum and alcohol prevented the Brontës from having an additional literary star in the family. Branwell Brontë, brother of the famous Brontë sisters, was a talented painter and poet, but his addictions led him to irrational and sometimes dangerous behavior. He eventually developed delirium tremens before dying of tuberculosis, leaving the world to wonder if he could have been more.

While opium was all the rage among the British literati, their French contemporaries preferred hashish. Charles Baudelaire put a stoner's twist on de Quincey with *Artificial Paradises* (1860). "The Poem of Hashish" includes the following description of the drug's effects:

First a certain absurd and irresistible hilarity comes over you. The most ordinary words, the most simple ideas take on a strange new aspect. This gaiety becomes insupportable to you, but it is useless to revolt. The demon has invaded you, all the efforts you make to resist only accelerate his progress.

Baudelaire met with Parisian writers like Honoré de Balzac, Alexandre Dumas, and Théophile Gautier for regular gatherings of "The Hashish Club" in the early 1840s at the Hôtel Pimodan. By all accounts, Baudelaire and Balzac didn't inhale, only attending for the conversation. As Baudelaire would later explain, for Balzac, "there is no deeper shame nor worse suffering for a man than to renounce control over his own will."

Did You Know?

Walt Whitman was also a famous abstainer. He rarely drank alcohol throughout his youth and claimed not to have touched strong liquor until he was thirty. One of his earliest works of fiction was the novel *Franklin Evans; or, The Inebriate* (1842), which promotes temperance—though years later he would denounce the book as "damned rot."

Balzac had a strong affinity for one substance: coffee. He is said to have thrown back fifty cups of black Turkish mud on a typical day, and wrote that, "Coffee is a great power in my life; I have observed its effects on an epic scale." Considering Balzac's prolific output, this level of caffeine consumption explains quite a bit. Dumas was no lightweight when it came to java, either, drinking dozens of cups a day and occasionally chewing on the raw grounds.

During the late nineteenth century, absinthe rose in popularity among writers like Oscar Wilde, Arthur Rimbaud, and Guy de Maupassant for its supposed hallucinogenic properties. The ritual of preparing it, from pouring the contents into a special reservoir glass to pouring water over a sugar cube set on a slotted spoon, offered the dramatic flair these writers sought in their substances. Wilde wrote of it:

> After the first glass, you see things as you wish they were. After the second, you see things as they are not. Finally, you see things as they really are, and that is the most horrible thing in the world.

Though only a handful of writers loved absinthe, many authors enjoyed, and suffered because of, alcohol over the years. Some of literature's most notorious drinkers include:

- Edgar Allan Poe—Though he managed to remain temperate for much of his life, the death of his wife in 1847 led to a downward spiral of whiskey and port, as he missed deadlines and embarrassed himself at public readings over his remaining years.

- Jack London—His autobiographical novel *John Barleycorn* (1913) describes in blunt detail how his alcoholism developed (beginning with a drunken episode at five years old) and how it came to define who he was.
- F. Scott Fitzgerald—Fitzgerald and his wife Zelda were serious drinkers and more serious partiers. They posted a list of house rules during one rager: "Visitors are requested not to break down doors in search of liquor, even when authorized to do so by the host and hostess. Weekend guests are respectfully notified that invitations to stay over Monday, issued by the host and hostess during the small hours of Sunday morning, must not be taken seriously."
- Dylan Thomas—After claiming that he'd had eighteen straight whiskies at his favorite New York City watering hole, the White Horse Tavern, Thomas passed out and never woke up for the hangover.

The Beats fully embraced drugs as their modern muse. Allen Ginsberg, William S. Burroughs, and Jack Kerouac experimented with alcohol, marijuana, Benzedrine, and morphine before adding LSD, peyote, amphetamines, and mescaline to their writing regimens.

Burroughs was a master of addiction literature, with most of his work, including *Naked Lunch* (1959) and *Junky* (1953), about getting high. His drug use was legendary: spending months touring South America in search of *yage*, selling heroin in Greenwich Village, and pawning his own typewriter to pay for his habit, requiring the author to handwrite his work. At one of his low points of morphine addiction, Burroughs wrote, "I had not taken a bath in a year nor changed my clothes or removed them except to stick a needle every hour in the fibrous grey wooden flesh of terminal addiction." Pretty nasty stuff.

As the Beats became beatniks and then hippies, a major influence in this period was Aldous Huxley's *The Doors of Perception* (1954), which followed in the tradition of de Quincey and Baudelaire, this time examining his experiences of an afternoon on mescaline.

Smoke 'Em if You Got 'Em

Though tamer than LSD and laudanum, tobacco has made some interesting appearances in the history of literature:

Renaissance poet and courtier Sir Walter Raleigh helped popularize tobacco in Europe. He brought it back with a tour of the New World and introduced it to the English court—supposedly even convincing Queen Elizabeth to have a smoke.

Mark Twain loved cheap cigars and smoked between twenty and forty a day, a habit started at eight years old. As he famously said, "To cease smoking is the easiest thing I ever did. I ought to know because I've done it a thousand times."

Though an ardent advocate for the widespread use of LSD and marijuana, Allen Ginsberg warned his readers against smoking in "Put Down Your Cigarette Rag (Don't Smoke)" as follows: "Don't Smoke Don't Smoke Nicotine Nicotine No / No don't smoke the official Dope Smoke Dope Dope."

With *Fear and Loathing in Las Vegas* (1972), Hunter S. Thompson broke from the high sense of cultural purpose offered by much of this drug literature. The semiautobiographical descriptions of excessive drug use and crazed antics make Huxley and de Quincey look conservative. But rather than encouraging drug use, it offered a satire of the "dope decade," with the protagonist reflecting that the hippie ethos was already on the wane and "the wave finally broke and rolled back."

From the look of things almost four decades later, Thompson seems to have been right. For the rest of the second half of the twentieth century, extended writings on drug use receded, and tended to be confined to "misery memoirs" and self-help works about overcoming addiction.

Perhaps the most notable work on addiction in recent decades is Irvine Welsh's *Trainspotting* (1993). Unlike most other works on drug use, his novel about Edinburgh heroin addicts is not told as a true or semitrue description of the author's own experiences (Welsh dabbled in petty crime as a youngster but straightened himself out before college). Perhaps concerned about his well-being or that being a junkie writer was just a bit too clichéd, Welsh seems to have put addiction literature in a healthier place for now: the fiction shelf.

WHY ARE THE BEST AUTOBIOGRAPHIES SO EMBARRASSING?

Humiliating confessions from St. Augustine to Augusten Burroughs

George Orwell once wrote that autobiography is "only to be trusted when it reveals something disgraceful. A man who gives a good account of himself is probably lying." This pointed comment gets to a surprising truth about the genre. While readers might expect to hear a grand life story of historical importance, the greatest works of memoir have focused far more on awkward tales of humiliation and shame.

St. Augustine began it all when he wrote his autobiography, *Confessions*, at the end of the fourth century. Written when the author was in his forties (he lived to be seventy-five), the work describes Augustine's wanton youth and episodes of suffering "the disease of lust which I preferred to satisfy rather than suppress."

Did You Know?

The actual word "autobiography" does not make its first appearance until 1797, when William Taylor suggested its use in the *Monthly Review* as a hybrid term of *autos* (self), *bios* (life), and *graphein* (write). He concluded it was too "pedantic," and it was not until 1809 that it was used in its present sense, by Robert Southey.

Augustine spends much of the work describing his various crimes and embarrassments (including stealing pears from a neighbor's tree) in salacious detail, before finally turning to God for redemption. *Confessions* puts self-exposure, rather than self-aggrandizement, at the center of autobiography, and offers a titillating—but ultimately moral—tale that the average reader can relate to. Augustine's formula worked so well that it was embraced by many writers in the genre.

Quick Quotes

"I dislike modern memoirs. They are generally written by people who have either entirely lost their memories, or have never done anything worth remembering."

—Oscar Wilde

"All those writers who write about their childhood! Gentle God, if I wrote about mine you wouldn't sit in the same room with me."

—Dorothy Parker

"I don't think anyone should write their autobiography until after they're dead."

—Samuel Goldwyn

The mystic Margery Kempe's *The Book of Margery Kempe* offered what is considered the first autobiography in the English language around 1420. Kempe's work reads like *Confessions* on psychedelics, complete with visions of Jesus and brutal persecution by religious leaders. These recollections may have been tragically true or merely reflections of her paranoia.

Autobiography really took off in the early seventeenth century, rising alongside the growing practice of journaling. John Bunyan, in *Grace Abounding to the Chief of Sinners* (1666), describes himself as "the very ringleader of all the youth that kept me company, in all manner of vice and ungodliness." Bunyan finds grace soon enough, but not before disclosing juicy bits about "lusts and fruits of the flesh." Sir Thomas Browne's revealing *Religio Medici* (1642)—a psychological self-portrait that examines the author's religious and scientific life—was one of the other major autobiographical works of the seventeenth century.

Over the next decades, the religious journey became less central to the genre, while the embarrassing details only became more important. The private diary of Samuel Pepys includes bits on his affair with a seventeen-year-old servant, as well as numerous respectable lady friends, but without the weighty sense of guilt of St. Augustine and the others brought to their accounts. While Jean-Jacques Rousseau's *Confessions* (1782) shares its name with St. Augustine's work (and includes admissions about stealing and siring five illegitimate children), it is framed in terms of worldly experiences rather than spiritual growth. One of the other successful memoirs of the period was the *Apology for the Life of Colley Cibber* (1740), which offered rambling and witty anecdotes on Cibber's life in the theater—a very different world than the church. (See Chapter 16).

Papa Shouldn't Preach

Rousseau wrote, "He who cannot fulfill the duties of a father has no right to become one." This is a strange selection of words considering that Rousseau and his partner Thérèse Levasseur had five illegitimate children, all of whom were placed in an orphanage. The woman running the orphanage supposedly berated Rousseau for his neglect and when he told her that he simply wasn't meant to be a father, she replied, "Then you must stop being one!"

Rousseau wrote of his autobiography that he "decided to make it a work unique in its unparalleled truthfulness," and as the genre exploded throughout the nineteenth century, candid emotion and intimacy continued to dominate it. William Wordsworth's autobiographical poem *The Prelude* (written at the not-quite-ripe age of twenty-eight) followed Rousseau's example in making the author's musings more important than external events.

A far more scandalous example of autobiography came in William Hazlitt's *Liber Amoris, or, The New Pygmalion* (1823). The book was written while the author was going through a painful divorce, and he wrote in the terms of a pining teenager his love for nineteen-year-old Sarah Walker, declaring: "Ah, Sarah! I am unworthy of your love," and, "frown if you will, I can bear your resentment for my ill behaviour, it is only your scorn and indifference that harrow up my soul." Hazlitt was roundly derided by critics for his adolescent emoting, but his disclosures were a landmark in raw, candid confession.

Other autobiographical writing of the century, including that of Benjamin Franklin, John Stuart Mill, John Ruskin, and Mark Twain avoided such outpourings, instead sticking with a more conversational and even didactic tone.

Did You Know?

In addition to writing his own autobiography, Mark Twain helped Ulysses S. Grant get a good deal on his. The Century Company offered Grant 10 percent royalties on his memoir—which would be expected to fetch him $20,000 to $30,000 (about $600,000 today). Twain intervened and connected the former president with Charles L. Webster & Co., which had published *Huckleberry Finn*, scoring Grant some $450,000 in royalties (more than $10.5 million by today's standards).

The twentieth century saw a snowballing of memoir writing, but things really kicked into high gear beginning in the 1950s as it became standard for someone in the public eye to write his or her life story. The 1960s marked the first time that celebrity autobiography overtook religious and spiritual autobiographies in sales.

Throughout these decades, past achievement was no longer a necessary prerequisite for writing one's life story, as writers like Robert Graves, Maya Angelou, and Maxine Hong Kingston actually started, rather than concluded, their careers with autobiographies. Recently there has been an onslaught of what book reviewer Sarah Goldstein calls "schtick lit," where writers undertake an unusual project specifically to write about it. Since Henry David Thoreau decided to spend some time in the woods and record his experiences, a raft of other stunt memoirs have come out. These include John Howard Griffin's *Black Like Me* (1961), in which the white author artificially darkens his skin and tours the segregated south, to A. J. Jacobs's *The Year of Living Biblically: One Man's Humble Attempt to Follow the Bible as Literally as Possible* (2008), and Pete Jordan's *Dishwasher: One Man's Quest to Wash Dishes in All Fifty States* (2007).

Perhaps the biggest trend in recent autobiography is what has been called the "memoir of crisis" or "misery lit," in which writers catalog their drug addictions, painful family histories, and all variety of other experiences from which they must recover. Works like Dave Pelzer's *A Child Called It* (1995), which recounts his

brutal abuse at the hands of his alcoholic mother, and Augusten Burroughs's tales of his chaotic childhood and struggle with alcoholism were huge bestsellers. In some ways the autobiography has come full circle, returning to St. Augustine's mission at the beginning of *Confessions*: "The recalling of my wicked ways is bitter in my memory, but I do it so that you will be sweet to me." Memoirists today might say the same, though "you" would no longer refer to God, but to the crowds at book signings and in Oprah's audience.

WHY COULDN'T F. SCOTT FITZGERALD WRITE A DECENT MOVIE?

Hollywood adaptations and why most novelists shouldn't quit their day jobs

Great novelists do not make great screenwriters. While this might seem counterintuitive (a great writer is a great writer, right?), the demands of Hollywood tend to rub novelists the wrong way. Though there are occasional exceptions (like Oscar winners John Irving and Mario Puzo), writing a fine book and writing a fine script often prove to be two very different talents.

This is not to say that great novels do not make great screenplays. Every year, dozens of films based on bestselling books or perennial classics are released, and many are critically acclaimed, get big box office returns, and occasionally both. From *Gone with the Wind* to *Slumdog Millionaire*, a whopping forty of the eighty-three winners of the Best Picture Oscar through 2010 have been based on books.

Quick Quotes

"It's like taking a cow and boiling it down to a bouillon cube."
—John Le Carré, on adapting his spy novels like *The Constant Gardener* and *The Tailor of Panama* into films.

"Movies have to pick their battles, and they have to pick fewer of them than novels do."
—Walter Kirn, on the adaptation of his novella *Up in the Air* (2001)

"[Hollywood] worships the visual image to the extent that it feels a need to constantly humiliate the purveyors of the written word."
—Gore Vidal

In the 1930s and 1940s, studio executives began thinking that star authors could command a similar loyalty at the box office as some of the big actors and actresses. They also expected that literary writers would add a richness and sophistication to the movies that the studios' hack writers couldn't match.

Attracted by the promise of easy money and a new platform where they could feature their work, a clutch of writers made a literary exodus to the west coast. William Faulkner, Aldous Huxley, Robert Benchley, Anthony Powell, Raymond Chandler, and Dorothy Parker all made their way to Hollywood and began trying to crank out screenplays. A few found success—Faulkner helped write the critically acclaimed *The Big Sleep* (1946); Parker helped write *A Star Is Born* (1937) and *Smash-up, the Story of a Woman*  (1947), both of which earned her Oscar nominations—but most found their work in Hollywood far less satisfying than their other writing, or hit a creative brick wall with the studios.

While deadline-oriented writers like Benchley and Parker, who had been writing for magazines like *The New Yorker* and *Vanity Fair*, could make the system work for them, for many authors it was just too stifling. The playwright Lillian Hellman said about working on the screenplay for *The Chase* (1966) that, "decision by majority vote is a fine form of government, but it's a stinking way to create." In *The Hollywood Studios*, Ethan Mordden gets at the trouble many writers faced in commenting on an original script by F. Scott Fitzgerald. He says that the author, "giv[es] too much of minor characters and too little of the principals. Words, words: yet little is conveyed. Nor does Fitzgerald have any grip on what Hollywood wants, what movies do."

Not knowing "what movies do" has been a challenge for many writers. While studios became less interested in literary types after these first experiments, embarrassments continued as writers tried their hand at filmmaking or got creatively involved

From Page to Screen

Among the authors who have made attempts to cross over to the big screen:

- F. Scott Fitzgerald—Made two tours through Hollywood, producing thousands of pages of scripts, but ended up with only one writing credit: for the 1938 film *Three Comrades,* received coolly by reviewers and audiences. The director Billy Wilder, a friend of Fitzgerald's, compared the writer to "a great sculptor who is hired to do a plumbing job."

- Aldous Huxley—Wrote the original screenplay for Disney's *Alice in Wonderland*, which was rejected for being too literal. While he had success adapting *Pride and Prejudice* and *Jane Eyre*, Huxley's efforts on two productions of his own *Brave New World* both ended without the film ever getting made.

- Nathanael West—Wrote more screenplays than he did novels, including *Five Came Back* starring Lucille Ball. Though the alienation and emptiness with which he depicts Hollywood in *The Day of the Locust* (1939) speaks volumes about his thoughts on the place.

- Anthony Powell—Went to Hollywood in 1937 to write screenplays, but left without a single credit to his name.

in the adaptations of their novels. Norman Mailer wrote five unre-markable screenplays, with *The New York Times* describing the adaptation of his novel *Tough Guys Don't Dance* (1984), which he wrote and directed, as "a celebration of the energy, the chutzpah, the imagination and, frequently, the misjudgment of Mr. Mailer." While Michael Cunningham wrote the screenplay to *A Home at the End of the World* (2004), which was received unenthusiastically by critics and made little money

at the box office, he did not do the writing on the adaptation of another of his novels, *The Hours* (2002), which was both a commercial and critical success.

There may be no better example of the dangers of author involvement than Stephen King, whose work has served as source material for dozens of films or television series (he and Zane Grey are neck and neck for most adapted authors, each with 116 adaptations according to the Internet Movie Database at the time of this writing). But while his work has been the source material for some film classics, there is something of a reverse relationship between King's involvement in a movie and the quality of the film. In

2004, film critic Erik Lundegaard rounded up the five best and five worst Stephen King adaptations (excluding TV movies) for MSN. See if you can spot a pattern:

BEST:	
1. *The Shawshank Redemption* (1994)	Didn't write screenplay
2. *The Dead Zone* (1983)	Didn't write screenplay
3. *The Shining* (1980)	Didn't write screenplay
4. *Misery* (1990)	Didn't write screenplay
5. *Stand by Me* (1986)	Didn't write screenplay
WORST:	
1. *Maximum Overdrive* (1986)	Wrote screenplay *and* directed
2. *Sleepwalkers* (1992)	Wrote screenplay
3. *Pet Sematary* (1989)	Wrote screenplay
4. *Graveyard Shift* (1990)	Didn't write screenplay
5. *Silver Bullet* (1985)	Wrote screenplay

Jonathan Franzen may have the healthiest attitude toward Hollywood. After selling the rights to *The Corrections* even before it was published, he told *Poets & Writers* magazine in 2002 that, "I know too much about Hollywood—about Hollywood adaptations of novels, about novelists interfacing with Hollywood—to have hopes of anything much besides getting paid. My chief hope is that a movie of *The Corrections* gets made but not before the option has been lucratively renewed a few times." Being in it for the money never sounded so wise.

Flipping the Script

While adaptations traditionally go from the page to the screen, they can also go the other direction. The classics *2001: A Space Odyssey*, by Arthur C. Clarke, and *The Third Man*, by Graham Greene, began as screenplays and were later novelized.

ARE SHORT STORY WRITERS LESS MATURE THAN NOVELISTS?

Why size matters, and when a novella is really just a novel

When it comes to literature, size matters. Whether it is a short story or massive novel, the length of a work has a lot to do with how we define and appreciate it. It may also tell us quite a bit about the character of the author him- or herself.

Hemingway is famous for his terseness, and he is not only the author of the shortest novel ever to win the Pulitzer Prize (*The Old Man and the Sea*) but also the author of what some have called the shortest novel ever written: "For sale: baby shoes, never worn."

Fighting Words

Faulkner and Hemingway had different views on the importance of length. Faulkner commented that Hemingway "had never been known to use a word that might send the reader to the dictionary." Hemingway retorted, "Poor Faulkner. Does he really think big emotions come from big words? He thinks I don't know the ten-dollar words. I know them all right. But there are older and simpler and better words, and those are the ones I use."

On the other end of the spectrum, Samuel Richardson is responsible for what is considered the longest novel in the English canon, with *Clarissa* (1748) coming in at around one million words. Even this may seem modest when compared to sequence novels like Anthony Powell's *Dance to the Music of Time* and Anthony Trollope's *Palliser* series, both of which weigh in at around two million words.

The king of the long book is Marcel Proust, whose *In Search of Lost Time* (also translated as *Remembrance of Things Past*), extends an estimated three million words in its seven volumes. The semiautobiographical novel, considered one of the first modernist novels, was published in France between 1913 and 1927.

Book length is often a case of form following function. During the late fifteenth century, books were kept short, often in the form of cheap "block books" printed as woodcuts, which were cheaper than printed books, so that the limited numbers of the literate public could actually afford them. As Gutenberg's moveable type became the norm and printing and buying books became less expensive, their size quickly grew. During the nineteenth century, the triple-decker novel was the standard format: this method divided lengthy works of 150–200,000 words (about 900 pages) into three books, allowing booksellers to charge for each part. Writing long was also the best option for writers like Charles Dickens and Thomas Hardy who were producing their works in serialized form. The longer they wrote, the more money they made.

Did You Know?

Each installment of Dickens's serialized novels ran as thirty-two pages of text, with sixteen pages of advertising and two engraved illustrations. The only exceptions were the final installments, which were twice this size. Going out with a bang (as in the noise the book makes when you drop it) has continued to this day, with series including *The Lord of the Rings* and *Twilight* saving the longest volume for last.

In his decades of publishing novels in monthly and weekly magazines, Dickens only missed one deadline: in May 1837, his beloved sister-in-law Mary Hogarth died, causing an interruption in the publication of both *The Pickwick Papers* and *Oliver Twist*, which were running in two separate publications.

As for modern publishing practices, bigger can still translate to better for the average publisher and book buyer. As the cost for binding books has gotten less expensive, adding a few hundred more pages to a book is a great way to entice readers to buy. The first long novel to top the best-seller list was the 1,200-page *Anthony Adverse* (1933) by Hervey Allen, which was advertised as "three books for the price of one."

This trend was still going strong in the twenty-first century, as Karen Holt observed in a 2004 article in *Publishers Weekly*: "Whether it's a debut novel or a veteran writer's swan song, the style for fall is unmistakable. Out: the little gem. In: the sprawling epic." Holt pointed to the release of doorstops like Tom Wolfe's *I Am Charlotte Simmons* (608 pages) and Susanna Clarke's *Jonathan Strange & Mr. Norrell* (800 pages), but massive tomes continue to weigh down the "new arrivals" tables at bookstores throughout the country.

Edgar Allan Poe was no fan of lengthy works, preferring to write short stories, or "tales," that could be read in one sitting.

In a famous critique published in *Graham's Magazine*, he calls the novel "objectionable" because of its length and argues that a tale allows that, "During the hour of perusal the soul of the reader is at the writer's control. There are no external or extrinsic influences—resulting from weariness or interruption." He states that while writing something too short is a problem, "undue length is yet more to be avoided."

Poe's points seem fair enough, but critic Clayton Hamilton argues in his classic work, *A Manual of the Art of Fiction* (1918), that the difference between short story writers and novelists might have more to do with the author's maturity than an aesthetic choice. He writes:

> The great novelists have all been men of mature years and accumulated wisdom. But if an author knows one little point of life profoundly, he may fashion a great short-story, even though that one thing be the only thing he knows.

Hamilton calls out Poe specifically, saying that while he wrote some of the finest and most visceral short stories in literature, the author "knew nothing" of what life is actually like and how people actually treat one another. Fellow writers certainly would seem to agree with Hamilton's assessment. T. S. Eliot accused Poe of having "the intellect of a highly gifted person before puberty," while W. H. Auden called him "an unmanly sort of man whose love life seems to have been largely confined to crying in laps and playing mouse."

Franz Kafka, a depressive who had his own troubles communicating with people, was primarily a writer of short stories. Hamilton also points to writers like Rudyard Kipling and Nathaniel

Hawthorne, who wrote some of their best short stories as young men and did not tackle novels until later in life. Of course, while it's an interesting idea, this theory fails to account for the experienced, apparently well-adjusted short story writers like Alice Munro or George Saunders or the many troubled and arguably immature novelists we do not need to name here.

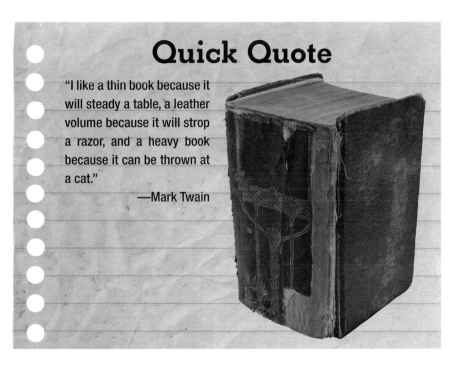

Quick Quote

"I like a thin book because it will steady a table, a leather volume because it will strop a razor, and a heavy book because it can be thrown at a cat."

—Mark Twain

It also does not stake a claim for writers of the novella—the long short story or short novel, depending on your perspective. This literary form, established by Giovanni Boccaccio's *Decameron* (c.1353), was referred to by Stephen King as, "an ill-defined and disreputable literary banana republic," and the parameters of a novella do indeed vary depending on whom you ask. A sample of official definitions put the minimum and maximum word length

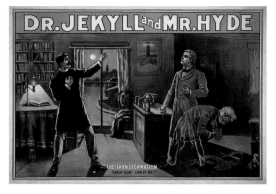

at anywhere from 10,000 to 70,000 words.

The Man Booker Prize has regularly had to address the difference between a novel and novella. Its rules officially state that the prize goes to "the best, eligible, full-length novel of the year." The judges got an earful in 2007 when Ian McEwan's *On Chesil Beach*, which is a mere 38,000 words long, was short-listed for the prize. When some questioned the choice, McEwan demurred, "That's their problem, not mine, I think."

Something of the Rodney Dangerfield of literary forms, the novella rarely gets credit. Classic novellas like Robert Louis Stevenson's *The Strange Case of Dr. Jekyll and Mr. Hyde* (25,906 words) and John Steinbeck's *Of Mice and Men* (a measly 19,352) are regularly described as novels, while Henry James's *The Turn of the Screw* and James Joyce's *The Dead* are more likely to fall into the short story category. Masters of the novella, such as James (*Daisy Miller, The Beast in the Jungle*), Steinbeck (*The Red Pony, The Pearl*), and Herman Melville (*Billy Budd* and *Bartleby, the Scrivener*) are better known as great novelists.

This might be due to the fact that the novella remains an indistinct literary form, or just that "novella-ist" does not really roll off the tongue. Whatever the case, at least no one is accusing them of knowing nothing about life.

Get to the Point

Edith Wharton recalled a time when she and Henry James were driving and stopped to ask for directions. "My good man," James said to a stranger, "to put it to you in two words, this lady and I have just arrived here from Slough; that is to say, to be more strictly accurate, we have recently *passed through* Slough on our way here, having actually motored to Windsor from Rye, which was our point of departure; and the darkness having overtaken us, we should be much obliged if you would tell us where we are in relation, say, to the High Street, which, as you of course know, leads to the Castle, after leaving on the left hand and turn down to the railway station." Sensing a need to simplify things, Wharton told the man they were just looking for King's Road. "Ye're in it," he said.

HOW DO YOU WRITE THE GREAT AMERICAN (OR BRITISH OR FRENCH) NOVEL?

Writing habits of the greats

"**W**hat is written without effort is in general read without pleasure," Samuel Johnson said. Readers generally only see the final product of the great works: edited, refined, and set down in its completed form. The "effort" authors put into composing their works offers plenty of fascinating anecdotes and insights about the writers and their craft, and offers those looking to write their own works suggestions for what it takes to write a great book.

For one thing, a consistent schedule is vital. Walter Mosley advocates writing every day, no matter what, stating that, "You don't go to a well once but daily. You don't skip a child's breakfast or forget to wake up in the morning. Sleep comes to you each day, and so does the muse." John Updike, an extremely prolific writer, was similarly forceful about the importance of working the writing muscles on a daily basis: "A day when I have produced nothing printable, when I have not gotten any words out, is a day lost and damned."

The timing of regular writing sessions can vary. Some write first thing in the morning—Toni Morrison begins before dawn and writes for a few hours, while Isaac Asimov got started at 7:30 in the morning and continued until 10 at night. Kingsley Amis was hardly as much of a writeaholic, grudgingly making his way to the typewriter around 10:30 in the morning, still in pajamas. Flaubert wrote at night and got moving at 10 in the morning.

Some writers break their days into word counts. Ian McEwan holds himself to a minimum of 500 words a day, telling the *Daily Mail*, "If I write twice that, I'm happy. By the middle of the week I'll have lost sight of whether it's good, bad or indifferent. All you have is quantity. So the word count acquires a ridiculous value." Other word count regimens include:

Ernest Hemingway	500 words/day
Jack London	1,000 words/day

W. Somerset Maugham	1,000 words/day
George Bernard Shaw	1,000 words/day
Norman Mailer	1,500 words/day
Anthony Trollope	3,000 words/day
Thomas Wolfe	10,000 words/day

James Joyce prided himself on quality over quantity. The story goes that when a friend asked if he'd had a good day writing, Joyce replied that he'd written three sentences—a good day for him indeed.

Then there are the epic writing session's when deadlines loom or inspiration hits. Alexandre Dumas bet a friend that he could write the entire first volume of *Le Chevalier de Maison Rouge* in three days. Downing huge amounts of coffee, he got out 34,000 words with time left on the  clock. Jack Kerouac is one of the most famous speed-writers, producing the entire text of *On the Road* in three weeks, writing at about 100 words a minute. Capote famously commented on Kerouac's writing style: "That's not writing, that's typing."

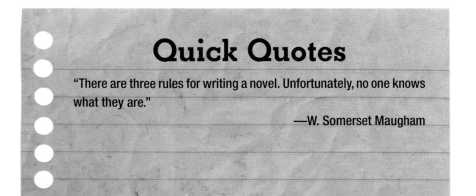

Quick Quotes

"There are three rules for writing a novel. Unfortunately, no one knows what they are."

—W. Somerset Maugham

What authors do when they are not writing can also play a role in their productivity. The Romantic poets regularly took walks to experience the outdoors, whether Coleridge and Wordsworth taking in the beauty of the Lake District, or Keats exploring Winchester, inspiring his poem "To Autumn." Henry David Thoreau admitted that he "cannot preserve my health and spirits, unless I spend four hours a day at least . . . sauntering through the woods and over the hills and fields." Joyce Carol Oates is an advocate of outdoor exercise as well, writing that, "The structural problems I set for myself in writing, in a long, snarled, frustrating and sometimes despairing morning of work, for instance, I can usually unsnarl by running in the afternoon."

Another type of motion was preferable to Henry James, who would pace about his home in East Essex while dictating his novels to a secretary, who tapped them onto the page with a Remington typewriter. The sound of the typewriter served as a rhythm for James to follow, and he reported finding it almost impossible to find his flow when the machine was in the shop and a replacement was brought in.

Just My Type

- Mark Twain claims to have been the first to use a typewriter to compose a novel. In a 1905 essay, "The First Typing Machine," he states: "I will now claim—until dispossessed—that I was the first person in the world to apply the type-machine to literature. That book must have been *The Adventures of Tom Sawyer.*" (Historians debate whether Friedrich Nietzsche was the first to use a typewriter. The philosopher is said to have used it to help soothe his migraines and growing blindness.)

- Gertrude Stein refused to learn to type and instead did her writing long-hand, dashing out a page every couple minutes, rarely going back and revising them before they were tran-scribed by a typist. This speed did not mean she was particularly prolific—she usually wrote for less than a half hour a day.

- Jack London had his own problems with the type-writer. As he wrote in his memoir, *John Barleycorn* (1913), his brother-in-law used the typewriter during the day, while London got use of it during the nights. Few in the household were likely to fall asleep with the banging London describes having to do on it: "The keys of that machine had to be hit so hard that to one outside the house it sounded like distant thunder or some one breaking up the furniture. I had to hit the keys so hard that I strained my first fingers to the elbows, while the ends of my fingers were blisters burst and blistered again. Had it been my machine I'd have operated it with a carpenter's hammer."

Philip Roth enjoys pacing as well, writing at his lectern as the words come to him, and a standing position has been surprisingly common for many writers as they worked. Hemingway, always a man ready for action, declared that, "Writing and travel broaden your ass if not your mind and I like to write standing up." Charles Dickens, Lewis Carroll, and Virginia Woolf wrote standing up as well, while the seven-foot-tall Thomas Wolfe actually used the top of his refrigerator as a desk.

On the other hand, some prefer a more relaxed approach: Truman Capote considered himself "a completely horizontal author," who preferred writing in bed. Marcel Proust and Mark Twain did their work lying down as well. Gustave Flaubert was more traditional, writing to his protégé Guy de Maupassant, "One cannot think and write except when seated." Roald Dahl not only liked to sit in a comfy chair, but generally wore a sleeping bag around his legs for warmth and comfort.

The habits of the great writers are as individual as their works, but they share the common theme that skill comes from sticking with the craft, and learning what works by unrelentingly putting "black on white" as de Maupassant called it. David Foster Wallace, writing to Don DeLillo in 1995, expressed his admiration for the author,

as well as his own frustration with the process: "Maybe I want a pep-talk, because I have to tell you I don't enjoy this war one bit."

DeLillo sympathized with Wallace's frustrations, responding that, "Over time I began to understand, one, that I was lucky to be doing this work, and, two, that the only way I'd get better at it was to be more serious, to under-stand the rigors of novel-writing and to make it central to my life . . . there's no trick of meditation or self-mastery that brought it about. I got older, that's all. I was not a born novelist (if anyone is). I had to grow into novelhood."

PART II

READERS

Why audiences love, hate, or ignore
the great works of literature

CAN BIG BOOK SALES LEAD TO MASS SUICIDE?

The history of bestsellers from John Bunyan to Dan Brown

The bestseller list is a crazy place. It is a rare thing in literature for a critically lauded work like Jonathan Franzen's *The Corrections* to be placed next to pulpy potboilers by John Grisham and James Patterson, as happened in 2001. Or for J. D. Salinger and John Steinbeck to appear alongside the sensationalistic writing of Harold Robbins, as they did in 1961. Quantity matters above all else on the bestseller list, and this has led to an interesting history since literary hits began to be tracked.

Though hardly what would be called a bestseller by today's standards, the earliest widespread success in England after the popularization of the Gutenberg press was John Bunyan's *Pilgrim's Progress* (1678), which sold 10,000 copies in its first year (it has since sold millions).

Did You Know?

Religious subjects continue to be a hot topic for big-selling books, at least in America. A number of books featuring Christ and his apostles have done well in the United States but not in England, including Lew Wallace's *Ben-Hur* (1886), Lloyd C. Douglas's *The Big Fisherman* (1942) and *The Robe* (1943), and Jerry B. Jenkins and Tim LaHaye's *Left Behind* series.

While Bunyan's Christian allegory remained a standard text in many English households for decades, the next book to ignite the popular imagination was the decidedly secular *Robinson Crusoe* (1719), which ran through four editions within its first year, followed by Swift's *Gulliver's Travels* (1726). The strong sales of these books were helped by the fact that they appealed to a broad range of readers, including adults and children.

As reading grew in popularity, the number of books sold also grew. Voltaire's *Candide* (1759) sold more than 20,000 copies in its first month, while Jean Jacques Rousseau's *Julie, ou la nouvelle Héloïse* posted similar sales two years later. Other hits included Samuel Richardson's *Pamela* (1740), followed by the gothic successes of Horace Walpole's *The Castle of Otranto* (1764) and Ann Radcliffe's *The Mysteries of Udolpho* thirty years after that.

What's in a Name?

On the nonfiction bestseller lists, books about pets, health (particularly dieting), medical tips, and history books on the American Civil War and World War II sell reliably well. When asked how to write a bestseller, Random House founder Bennett Cerf suggested simply titling the work *Lincoln's Doctor's Dog.*

Lulu.com attempted a more scientific (though admittedly flawed) study of what tops the list, in 2005. The company used a computer model to evaluate what attributes (including number of words and whether titles contained the names of places or people) appear in the titles of #1 *New York Times* bestsellers between 1955 and 2004. It determined that with its abstract words and short title, Agatha Christie's *Sleeping Murder* (#1 in 1976) was perfectly phrased to ensure big sales. Literal titles like the *Harry Potter* books or *The Da Vinci Code* did not score as well.

With the sale of pirated versions of these works rampant, it was impossible to get accurate sales numbers. Spin-offs and translations helped stoke the popularity of existing works, with

Robinson Crusoe alone being a source of some 700 alternate versions over the decades after its first publication. Johann Wolfgang von Goethe's bestselling novel *The Sorrows of Young Werther* (1774), led to spin-offs like porcelain puppets, jewelry, and Werther *eau de cologne.*

A less pleasing by-product of the work's success was the "Werther effect," as young men throughout Europe not only emulated the style and dress of the young artist at the center of the story, but also followed his example by killing themselves. As numerous reports of suicide across Europe followed the publication of Goethe's book, several countries banned the novel. The author Christoph Friedrich Nicolai took perhaps a more constructive (and profitable) approach by writing *The Joys of Young Werther* (1775), which gave the story a happy ending.

As literacy expanded and the costs of buying and borrowing books decreased, Lord Byron's *Don Juan* (1819) and Sir Walter Scott's Waverley novels marked the beginning of true bestsellers as we understand them today. In the nineteenth century a top seller could expect to sell 50,000 copies.

Can a Book be Too Much of a Bestseller?

In 2008, after appearing on *The New York Times* bestseller list for eighty consecutive weeks, thanks to its selection for the *Oprah* Book Club, Elie Wiesel's *Night* (1960) was abruptly dropped from the list. Public Editor Clark Hoyt explained that, "The *Times*'s news survey department, which compiles the list, decided the Holocaust memoir wasn't a new bestseller but a classic like *Animal Farm or To Kill a Mockingbird*, which sell hundreds of thousands of copies a year largely through course adoptions. . . . We simply cannot track such books indefinitely."

The first bestseller list appeared in the industry journal *Bookman* in 1895 (only listing fiction) and seventeen years later *Publishers Weekly* introduced the first list for nonfiction books. Over the following decades, dozens more papers and outlets began their own weekly or monthly charts of the top-selling books, with *The New York Times* finally adopting its list in 1942. Less enthusiastic than Americans about having books compete with one another, the British held off on any sort of formal list until the 1970s, when *The Bookseller* and the *Sunday Times* introduced theirs.

These lists tracked a stream of major hits that held on to the top spot week after week, from Erich Maria Remarque's *All Quiet on the Western Front* (1929) to Margaret Mitchell's *Gone with the Wind* (1936), which sold a million copies within its first few months of publication. The paperback revolution that began in 1935 and exploded in the 1960s gave an extra jolt to the numbers for hits like Mario Puzo's *The Godfather* (1969), Erich Segal's *Love Story* (1970), and Peter Blatty's *The Exorcist* (1971).

All of the above-mentioned books also had massive movie adaptations that helped further propel their sales, reflecting the growing role that marketing and cross-promotion have come to play in ensuring bestseller status. The making of a blockbuster book had quickly become a science for major publishers, based on an increasingly well-defined set of marketing techniques to help ensure a hit. Some combination of Dan Brown, Tom Clancy, Patricia Cornwell, Janet Evanovich, John Grisham, James Patterson, and Nicholas Sparks have been responsible for an average of six of the ten bestselling books every year for the past decade.

Despite this predictability, there are still the stories of small presses or unknown authors having huge success. Canongate paid Yann Martel £3,000 for *The Life of Pi* before it took home a cartload of literary prizes and sold a million copies for its Scottish publisher. J. K. Rowling was paid the same for her first Harry Potter book with Bloomsbury.

Bestselling Scandals

Sometimes marketing efforts can go too far. In the 1980s, the Scientology movement was accused of pumping up the sales numbers of founder L. Ron Hubbard's books so they would appear on *The New York Times* list.

In the mid-1990s, the consulting firm that employed the authors of the business book *The Discipline of Market Leaders* bought tens of thousands of copies from retailers, so they could give the books to their clients and garner some buzz by making the bestseller list. Though these efforts were considered unethical, they were not illegal and certainly got the book press, though it might not have been the kind the authors had hoped.

Sarah Palin's blockbuster *Going Rogue* (2009) was accused of something similar when it was revealed that her political action committee had spent $63,000 buying copies of her own book to give to donors. Considering the book went on to sell 2.6 million copies, that was just a drop in the bucket.

Big sales have certainly not meant longevity for many bestselling titles, as many are forgotten as soon as they drop off the list. Critics have derided the low quality of writing in many of the works, complaining that works of predictable genre fiction with simple characters and writing are the most likely to be devoured by the public, decade after decade. In *Junk Fiction: America's Obsessions with Bestsellers* (2009), S. T. Joshi looks over a list of the fifteen books that have sold more than seven million copies, and concludes that, excluding *To Kill a Mockingbird* (1960) and two Orwell novels:

> Not a single work is anything but a potboiler. . . .
> They are, in effect, inferior works embodying certain
> recognized flaws that doom them to insignificance,

and their popularity during their heyday was based largely upon their hitting a popular nerve and—one might as well come out and say it—their appeal to a broad mass of ill-educated and uncultivated readers.

Zing! With reviews like this, it's no wonder that many best-selling authors prefer to worry less about their canonization and more about their cash flow. John Grisham, who's had the top-selling book of the year nine times since 1994, said, "Life is much simpler ignoring reviews and the nasty people who write them. Critics should find meaningful work." Danielle Steel offered a lighter defense, saying, "A bad review is like baking a cake with all the best ingredients and having someone sit on it."

Mickey Spillane, the crime writer who in 1980 had written seven of the top fifteen all-time bestselling fiction titles in America, was one of the most unapologetic proponents of commercial litera-ture. Among his ripostes:

- "There are more salted peanuts consumed than caviar."
- "I have no fans. You know what I got? Customers."
- "Inspiration is an empty bank account."

It should be no surprise that Ayn Rand was a fan.

Can these writers be defended from a literary perspective? Writing in *The Spectator* in 2007, journalist Tony Parsons did his best to mount a sympathetic defense of bestselling authors. He declared that every blockbuster comes from a place of passion and often after years of struggling through flops. "Anything that gets on to the bestseller list deserves to be there. And even if it is not your cup of Darjeeling, never doubt that the

author of *The Da Vinci Code* is as serious in his intent as the author of *Atonement.*" Perhaps the Pattersons and Browns of the world deserve an "A" for effort, in addition to their enviable royalty checks.

Best-selling books of all time

1. *The Bible*	5,000+ million
2. *Quotations from Chairman Mao Zedong* by Mao Zedong	900 million
3. *The Qur'an*	800 million
4. *Xinhua Zidian*	400 million
5. *The Book of Mormon* by Joseph Smith, Jr.	120 million
6. *Harry Potter and the Sorcerer's Stone* by J. K. Rowling	107 million
7. *And Then There Were None* by Agatha Christie	100 million
8. *The Lord of the Rings* by J. R. R. Tolkien	100 million
9. *Harry Potter and the Half-Blood Prince* by J. K. Rowling	65 million
10. *The Da Vinci Code* by Dan Brown	65 million

Source: Publications International, Ltd.

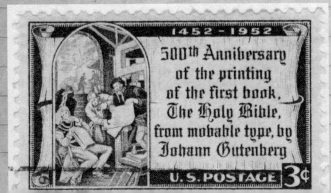

WHY DON'T TODAY'S WRITERS HAVE AS MANY GROUPIES AS LORD BYRON?

The rise and fall of literary celebrity

Before there were rock stars or movie stars, there were literary stars. Gossiped about, adored by fans, and featured on the covers of magazines, famous authors were at the pinnacle of the celebrity world for a good part of the nineteenth century and into the twentieth. As the first mass-media celebrities, authors had to navigate uncharted waters as they figured out how to mold their public image, striking a balance between artistic integrity and naked self-promotion. By the 1970s, artistic integrity won out, ending the era of the literary star with a whimper.

If there was one man who blazed the trail for national literary stardom, it was Lord Byron. The publication of *Childe Harold's Pilgrimage* (1812–18) brought him massive attention from the burgeoning press and general public, curious about the man behind the verses. Byron cultivated a public image as the sort of brooding and passionate "Byronic hero" found in his poetry.

When having portraits done, Byron would instruct artists to portray him as a "man of action," without a pen or book in hand (more images of Byron remain than any of his fellow Romantics). His friend Lady Blessington commented on his behavior in a letter: "There was no sort of celebrity he did not, at some period or other, condescend to seek, and he was not over nice in the means, provided he obtained it in the end."

There was also no sort of smitten fan that he did not pursue. Bedding men, women, boys, and girls, Byron's sexual appetite was notorious. His wife, Annabella, coined the phrase "Byromania" to describe the adulation he received from admirers, sardonically describing, "how all the women were absurdly courting him and trying to deserve the lash of his Satire." No wonder their marriage only lasted two years.

Fame was something Byron reflected on frequently, making such statements as:

- "Fame is the thirst of youth."
- "What is fame? The advantage of being known by people of whom you yourself know nothing, and for whom you care as little."
- "Folly loves the martyrdom of fame."

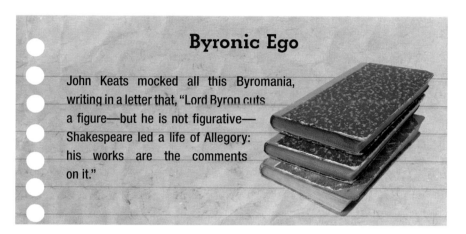

Byronic Ego

John Keats mocked all this Byromania, writing in a letter that, "Lord Byron cuts a figure—but he is not figurative—Shakespeare led a life of Allegory: his works are the comments on it."

Byron was just the most visible face in what was a burgeoning literary celebrity culture. Other Romantics, especially Keats, Shelley, and Elizabeth Barrett Browning, received fan letters and requests for autographs and souvenirs at a level not seen before. Fans would even imitate their dress and mannerisms. In a time where books were one of the only forms of mass media, authors commanded much attention.

Of course, this celebrity worship could create some tension with authors' desire to be taken seriously. Critics have suggested that Byron's credibility as a poet was undermined by his celebrity with the masses, and indeed, these days more readers are likely to know of Byron than read his poetry.

This was encouraged and complicated by the changing nature of the book-publishing market. As literature became more commercialized, authors were brought into the advertising and publicity of their works. Authorship could come very close to entrepreneurship, with the writer's personality serving as a major selling point.

One of the major platforms for promoting an author was the lecture circuit, and if Byron's swagger made him something of the Elvis of literary celebrity, Charles Dickens was a Beatle, bringing a British invasion to America during his two reading tours across the country. During his first, in 1842, the author was greeted by newspaper editors jockeying for an exclusive interview when his ship pulled into Boston Harbor.

Dickens's audiences wanted more than just to hear him read, as summarized in a Dublin newspaper: "Nowadays the public must know all about your domestic relations, your personal appearance, your age, the number of your children, the colour of your eyes and hair." Sound familiar?

These live performances were big business for Dickens—as well as the other two major celebrity authors of the nineteenth century, Mark Twain and Oscar Wilde—with fans waiting in line overnight, sold-out theaters, and big box-office receipts.

Like Byron before him, Twain deliberately cultivated an image of himself that was hard to separate from his work: that of the quintessential American, complete with a trademark costume of an all-white suit. Unlike Byron, Twain focused his appearances on humor and telling a good joke (he is considered by some to be America's first stand-up comic). A *New York Times* reviewer called Mark Twain's style "a quaint one, both in manner and method, and throughout his discourse he managed to keep on the right side of his audience and frequently convulsed it with hearty laughter." Newspapers and magazines helped feed the "event" status of these live shows.

Though the lecture circuit lost steam in America beginning in the 1880s, this coincided with a second wave of new periodicals and newspapers, including the inexpensive illustrated weeklies *Life* and later *Time*, which created a truly national media. These magazines featured profiles of the authors, with cover photos to tie them to their public personas—J. D. Salinger in a field of rye, T. S. Eliot among a surrealistic landscape of hands growing from the ground like trees.

Cover Boy

Ernest Hemingway is a favorite literary cover boy, gracing the front of *Time* twice and *Life* three times.

Many celebrated writers were hardly mainstream, with modernists like Eliot and Gertrude Stein grabbing their share of national attention. In 1934, Stein and her partner Alice B. Toklas returned to New York to be greeted by a revolving billboard in Times Square reading "Gertrude Stein has arrived in New York," before heading to Washington D.C. for tea with Eleanor Roosevelt

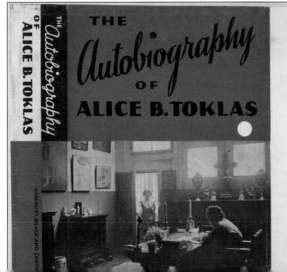

and on to Hollywood to rub elbows with Charlie Chaplain. As Loren Daniel Glass writes in *Authors Inc.*, "Few things are more striking about the primary spokespeople for modernism than the contrast between their stated theories of self-effacement and their actual practice and literary-historical destiny of self-aggrandizement and even shameless self-promotion."

Several other famous writers, including Edith Wharton, F. Scott Fitzgerald, and Ernest Hemingway, were frequently discussed in the media. As with earlier celebrity authors, Hemingway's press attention came from the perceived overlap of his life and his fictional writing, with much coverage of his dramatic adventures, including bullfights, African safaris, and reporting on the Spanish Civil War.

A Bit Sensitive

Hemingway cared deeply about what was said of him in the press, and in one famous instance went to blows with critic Max Eastman, who had written that Hemingway's *Death in the Afternoon* (1932) had the tone of a man "wearing false hair on his chest." Bumping into Eastman at his publisher's office, the author demanded they compare chests, and after mocking Eastman's relative hairlessness, slapped him in the face with a book. He told *The New York Times*, "I'll put up $1,000 for any charity he favors or for himself. Then we'll go into a room and he can read his book to me—the part of his book about me. Well, the best man unlocks the door."

Hemingway was truly larger than life, but unlike Byron or Twain, he had to compete for attention from a public that was becoming more interested in film and television stars. Following in Hemingway's legacy of hypermasculine braggadocio was Norman Mailer, who not only wrote critically acclaimed novels but also ran for mayor of New York, challenged professional boxers to fight, and sparked public feuds with other authors. He is believed to have been interviewed more times than any writer who has ever lived.

Success took its toll on Mailer. In his collection of commentary and short works *Advertisements for Myself* (1959), Mailer writes, "Success has been a lobotomy of my past," and, "I was a node in a new electronic landscape of celebrity, personality and status," and his apparent exhaustion with the whole enterprise reflected a significant shift in how big authors related to the public.

The next literary star in the succession should probably have been Philip Roth. His 1969 novel *Portnoy's Complaint* received much attention, with television hosts and tabloids discussing it as if, like Byron's Don Juan before him, the novel's hypersexed protagonist was simply an extension of its author. In interviews and appearances, Roth came across as a thoughtful, reserved intellectual, keeping interviews on serious, impersonal topics and avoiding the salacious details the mass market was hoping for.

It was the same with John Updike. His 1968 novel *Couples* became a number-one bestseller and landed him on the cover of *Time*, but Updike simply focused on his writing, gave genial interviews, and made little effort to play up his public persona. When Updike followed up his hit with the eight-hour closet drama, *Buchanan Dying*, he described it as, "an act of penance for a commercially successful novel set in New England." You weren't likely to catch Updike at a bullfight.

With rare exception, this trend has continued. Partly due to the changed media landscape, but perhaps also because publishing is an industry where literary merit and self-promotion tend to be seen as inversely proportionate, authors of the past several decades have generally avoided star status. The era of literary celebrity seems to have gone out with Norman Mailer.

The Anti-Celebrities

Literary stardom may not be what it used to be, but authors looking for attention might consider another way to get attention: avoid the spotlight completely. Authors such as Emily Dickinson, J. D. Salinger, and Thomas Pynchon fascinate readers not only because of their work but also because of the limited information anyone has about them. Pynchon offers an interesting example of a recluse who still likes to pop his head up now and then in often bizarre places:

- A 1976 article in *Soho Weekly* offered the theory that Pynchon was actually J. D. Salinger. The author wrote to the editors, "Not bad. Keep trying."
- After NBC's *The John Larroquette Show* made several references to him, Pynchon reached out to the show through his agent, offering a couple pointers, such as, "You call him Tom, and no one ever calls him Tom."
- He made two cameos on *The Simpsons*, one in which he sports a brown paper bag over his head shouting blurbs for Marge's book ("Thomas Pynchon loved this book, almost as much as he loves cameras!") and another where his lines are made

up of puns on his novel titles ("These wings are '*V*'-licious! I'll put this recipe in 'The *Gravity's Rainbow* Cookbook,' right next to 'The Frying of Latke 49.'"). This is one of only two times a recording of his voice has been released on a mainstream outlet.

- He wrote an amusing article in honor of the tenth anniversary of *The Daily Show with Jon Stewart*, which postulates that Stewart is actually the reincarnation of his evil TV exec character in *Death to Smoochy* (2002).

Critic Arthur Salm reflects that, "If Pynchon and Paris Hilton were ever to meet—the circumstances, I admit, are beyond imagining—the resulting matter/antimatter explosion would vaporize everything from here to Tau Ceti IV."

DID ROBINSON CRUSOE TEACH JAMES FREY TO LIE?

The long history of fake memoirs and literary hoaxes

James Frey made a huge splash in the literary world; first, when his Oprah-endorsed memoir *A Million Little Pieces* (2003) sold millions of copies, and more so when it was suddenly revealed to be little more than a tall tale of tough-guy exaggeration. Frey's epic flameout drew headlines, but it was far from the first literary hoax. Since the early days of novels, literature's greatest writers have tricked audiences into believing unbelievable stories, often for their own amusement.

Daniel Defoe's *Robinson Crusoe* (1719), which many consider to be the first novel in English, was presented as autobiography. He took pains to make it look like Crusoe's work, leaving his own name off the first edition, leading some to believe that Robinson Crusoe actually existed and that the story was true. The hack writer Charles Gildon (who was likely looking to get a little profits of his own from Defoe's impressive sales) actually went to the trouble of publishing *Robinson Crusoe Examin'd and Criticis'd* (1719), which accused Defoe of lying.

This wasn't a one-off for Defoe, and he followed it up with several other works that used the conventions of memoir to give his works a sense of authenticity, with the stories often presented as collections of letters or journals, including *Memoirs of a Cavalier* (1720), *Captain Singleton* (1720), and *Moll Flanders* (1722). Moll opens her book with a boast that sounds like something Frey might have made: "My true name is so well known in the [prison] records, or registers at Newgate, and in the Old-Baily . . . that it is not to be expected I should set my name, or the account of my family to this work." Defoe's *A Journal of the Plague Year* (1722) is written as a real account of London in 1665 during the Great Plague, discussing specific locations, casualty figures, and anecdotes to add credibility.

Quick Quotes

"I write fiction and I'm told it's autobiography, I write autobiography and I'm told it's fiction, so since I'm so dim and they're so smart, let them decide what it is or it isn't."

—Philip Roth

"People think that because a novel's invented, it isn't true. Exactly the reverse is the case. Biography and memoirs can never be wholly true, since they cannot include every conceivable circumstance of what happened. The novel can do that."

—Anthony Powell

"All autobiographies are lies. I do not mean unconscious, unintentional lies; I mean deliberate lies. No man is bad enough to tell the truth himself during his lifetime, involving, as it must, the truth about his family and friends and colleagues. And no man is good enough to tell the truth in a document which he suppresses until there is nobody left alive to contradict him."

—George Bernard Shaw

As the novel was beginning to evolve, the traditional categories of fiction and nonfiction were not easily distinguished, and writers sought only to tell a compelling story, putting it in terms that a reader would be familiar with—letters, journals, and autobiography. Henry Fielding, Samuel Richardson, Laurence Sterne, and John Cleland all wrote fiction in the form of autobiography, whether about women of society, criminals, or prostitutes.

Jonathan Swift's *Gulliver's Travels* (1726) was similarly attributed to Lemuel Gulliver, and framed as a true account of his voyages at sea,

though its fantastical situations made it unlikely to be mistaken for fact by the intelligent reader. Swift's essay "A Modest Proposal" (1729) was taken seriously by many readers, who missed his satirical point and believed he was actually recommending class-based cannibalism.

Horace Walpole published *The Castle of Otranto* (1764) under the pretense that it was a manuscript from the sixteenth century that had just been recently discovered. It was soon exposed, and Walpole indicated he was in fact the author in the book's second edition.

Who Are You Going to Believe?

In a later edition of Johann Wolfgang von Goethe's autobiography, an odd footnote appeared. Following the author's assertion, "With her, for the first time in my life, I really fell in love!," the editor added an asterisk and comment that "Here Goethe was in error."

As the novel became more firmly established, writers looking to take some poetic license turned to the newspaper. Edgar Allan Poe wrote a number of sensational, and completely fake, stories over a period of years which he presented as fact:

- The story of Hans Pfaall in an 1885 issue of *Southern Literary Messenger,* about a man in a balloon who dropped a note to onlookers that described his five years spent on the moon.
- Tales of the North Pole adventures and death of Arthur Pym, originally published as serialized news feature in the *Southern Literary Messenger,* would later come out as the novel *The Narrative of Arthur Gordon Pym* (1838).

- "The Great Balloon Hoax" about a famous balloonist who had flown across the Atlantic (at the time a first) in the *New York Sun.*
- During the 1849 gold rush, Poe published a story in *The Flag of Our Union* about a German chemist who had figured out how to transform lead into gold. He later described his amazement at the speed with which the newspapers were snatched up.

These inventions would have gotten Poe fired immediately today, but in the mid-nineteenth century, newspapers were extremely competitive and writers were encouraged to write the stories that would give them the edge over competitors, sacrificing complete accuracy if need be (Poe's own *Sun* editor is suspected of having invented the famous "Great Moon Hoax" of the same period, which described life on the moon complete with huge beavers and winged humans). It was believed to be the discerning reader's responsibility to call out the fake stories and those who were hoodwinked had only themselves to blame. No wonder that Poe later referred to this period as the "epoch of the hoax."

Pseudo-Science

More recent writers have used fake science to give their works an added narrative thrust. In *Enduring Love* (1997), a novel about a science writer, Ian McEwan included a fraudulent article from a fake medical journal. Many critics assumed the work was real and had

Mark Twain, working as a reporter at Nevada's *Territorial Enterprise* in the 1860s, played the same game, though his stories were less about science and adventure and more about blood and guts. He would later describe with amusement the "feats and calamities that we never hesitated about devising when the public needed matters of thrilling slaughter, mutilation and general destruction." His fake stories included accounts of a group of Native Americans who had suffocated in a tunnel, a petrified man found sitting upright in the mountains, and a father who scalped his wife and killed six of his children (described in graphic detail).

Choosing a lighter topic, H. L. Mencken tested his readers with his 1917 article, "A Neglected Anniversary" in the *New York Evening Mail*, which outlined a fictitious history of the bathtub in America. It explained that while there were major concerns with the invention, it was broadly embraced after President Millard Fillmore installed one in the White House in 1850.

Ralph Waldo Emerson stated that, "Truth is beautiful, without doubt; but so are lies." While authors have created some beautiful baloney in the past, it's hard to say if he would extend such kind words to Frey and the spate of other fake memoirists that have proliferated in recent years. Among them:

- JT LeRoy—Drug addicted, sexually confused male prostitute who made public appearances in an Andy Warhol wig and dark sunglasses. In fact it was sometime rock musician Laura Albert who wrote the memoirs and her close friend Savannah Knoop who posed in public.
- Margaret B. Jones—Alleged half-white, half–Native American woman writes about her life growing up as a foster child in Los Angeles gangs. She was in fact Margaret Seltzer, who grew up in the well-off Sherman Oaks, and was outed when her sister spotted a profile on her in *The New York Times.*
- Misha Levy Defonseca—Lost her parents in the Holocaust and trekked 2,000 miles searching for them, killing a Nazi soldier and being adopted by wolves—but was actually raised by a pack of loving grandparents in Belgium, safe from the terrors of World War II.

Nasdijj, Herman Rosenblat, Helen Darville, Michael Pellegrino, Anthony Godby Johnson . . . the list of recent memoir frauds goes on. Today's fake memoir craze may be only the latest in a grand tradition of literary cons. But LeRoy, Frey, and the other latter-day deceivers seem to lack what Swift, Twain, and Poe had in spades: a sense of humor. Perhaps that may explain why a humorist like David Sedaris, who openly acknowledges exaggerating elements of his bestselling memoirs, continues to sit comfortably on the nonfiction shelves. In the meantime it's the writers of overserious "misery lit" who have been publicly castigated and promptly tossed into the fiction section, if not the trash.

...even the plainest woman
into a beautiful dress
and unconsciously she
try to live up to it.

- Lady Duff Gordon

WHO'S AFRAID OF
JANE AUSTEN?
Novelists' battle for respectability

2009's *Pride and Prejudice and Zombies* was a bizarre twist on the Jane Austen classic, the original work may actually have been even more unsettling to critics two centuries earlier. At the time of its publication, *Pride and Prejudice* (1813) was lumped in with many other (often quite enjoyable) novels deemed to be "trash" by the cultural and religious authorities. The novel was a target of derision throughout its formative decades.

Before the nineteenth century, reading had largely been an aristocratic activity, restricted to a small segment of the population. This slowly shifted as individuals began to have more leisure time in which to read, and it became more affordable.

The increasing popularity was aided by "circulating libraries," established by publishers and literary societies, which took off toward the end of the eighteenth century. These served as something of a combination library and bookstore, where visitors could borrow books for a negligible price—a popular idea, because a book could cost as much as a week's salary for an average worker. By far the most popular works in these libraries were novels, and 70 to 80 percent of all books borrowed were fiction.

These libraries were subsequently mocked by the upper classes and elites as selling "trash literature," and critics complained that they degraded works of true value by offering mostly contemporary fiction and targeting women and lower-class readers. Fiction was not studied in universities, and novels were seen as merely an amusement or worse.

Did You Know?

Ome of the most vocal critics of novels and novel-reading was Samuel Taylor Coleridge, who stated in 1808 that, "where the reading of novels prevails as a habit, it occasions in time the entire destruction of the powers of the mind." He added that novel reading "is such an utter loss to the reader that it is not so much to be called pass-time as kill-time."

Novels were also attacked by religious critics, who felt the works' exciting content promoted superficial pleasure and titillation, rather than self-improvement. Novels were seen as causing corruption and immorality, and were even described as "poison" that could corrupt those who took them in. Some evangelicals contended that the Bible held support for their anti-fiction beliefs. Jane West, a conservative writer who was popular in her day, captures this negative attitude toward novels, a bit ironically, in her introduction to *The Infidel Father: A Novel* (1802), as she laments that the form is likely not going away, but could at least be used to more edifying ends:

> The rage for novels does not decrease; and, though I by no means think them the best vehicles for "the words of sound doctrine," yet, while the enemies of our church and state continue to pour their poison into unwary ears through this channel, it behooves the friends of our establishments to convey an antidote by the same course.

A notable hint of sexism can be sensed in these diatribes against novels. The majority of readers of fiction were women, with favorite books serving a special value in their social circles as they traded with one another. Critics derided the novels as "women's literature." As the Church of England's *Quarterly Review* condescendingly put it in 1842, trying to explain why the bulk of readers were women, "they are more naturally sensitive, more impressionable, than the other sex; and secondly, their engagements are of a less engrossing nature—they have more time to indulge in reveries of fiction."

Did You Know?

A s she was considering leaving her teaching career behind, Charlotte Brontë wrote to poet laureate Robert Southey asking if he thought she could earn a living as a writer. He responded: "Literature cannot be the business of a woman's life, and it ought not to be. The more she is engaged in her proper duties, the less leisure will she have for it."

The works of Jane Austen were lumped together with these "women's novels" and received little critical notice during her time, with none of her novels being reprinted until 1831. Ralph Waldo Emerson commented that her books, "seem to me vulgar in tone, sterile in artistic invention, imprisoned in their wretched conventions of English society, without genius, wit, or knowledge of the world. Never was life so pinched and narrow." Mark Twain offered that, "Jane Austen's books, too, are absent from this library. Just that one omission alone would make a fairly good library out of a library that hadn't a book in it."

All these protests took a toll on novelists. In *The Reading Lesson*, critic Patrick Brantlinger explains, "As a genre, the modern novel was born with an inferiority complex: it wasn't classical, it wasn't poetry, and it wasn't history." Novels began in a vague, ill-defined format, with writers making up the rules as they went along. There is a self-consciousness in many early novels, with writers satirizing the form, offering an acknowledgment of and something of an apology for its shortcomings.

In his essay "Novel Reading," Anthony Trollope points out the central role that novels had gained in popular literature, and in their ability to shape mass opinion. He writes that, "At different periods in our history, the preacher, the dramatist, the essayist, and the poet have been efficacious over others. . . . Now it is the novelist." The essay may sound like a full-throated defense of novels, but he adds, "There are reasons why we would wish it were otherwise. The reading of novels can hardly strengthen the intelligence."

Austen herself takes a more defensive stance for the novel in *Northanger Abbey*:

> Although our productions have afforded more extensive and unaffected pleasure than those of any other literary corporation in the world, no species of composition has been so much decried . . . there seems almost a general wish of decrying the capacity and undervaluing the labour of the novelist, and of slighting the performances which have only genius, wit, and taste to recommend them.

The idea that reading novels and romances can lead to delusion goes at least as far back as Don Quixote's misguided quests, and novelists as well as critics discussed how reading them could lead readers to believe they lived in a fantasy world. Characters like Austen's Catherine Morland in *Northanger Abbey* and Flaubert's Emma Bovary in *Madame Bovary* (1857) take ill-advised actions as a result of the books they read. In *The Picture of Dorian Gray* (1890), the title character epitomizes this through the impact that the "yellow book" that Lord Henry sends over has on him. He describes it as a "poisonous book. The heavy odour of incense seemed to cling about its pages and to trouble the brain," which leads him down a path of crime and self-destruction.

By the time *Dorian Gray* was published, novelists no longer had to hold their heads low. "The rage for novels" did not decrease, but expanded significantly throughout the nineteenth century, until novels were ubiquitous, essentially the only type of literary work read by the masses.

In order to make a living, most intelligent writers learned to work in this new format, whether they had a natural inclination for it or not. With this movement toward novels, even the highbrow reader was compelled to shift to these works. Courses on the novel were added to college curricula, critics began discussing the works without having to offer a disclaimer to readers, and the works of George Eliot, the Brontës, and Jane Austen were incorporated into the canon of English literature.

Women on Top

A study by Lulu.com found that women's share of the bestseller list is growing. Looking at the books that made it to #1 on *The New York Times* bestseller list over the fifty years from 1955 to 2008, the researchers found that while women's books only made up 17.8 percent of these for the first decade of the study (1955–1964), they were up to 46 percent for the last decade in the study (1995–2004). This is thanks in large part to the big sales of J. K. Rowling and Danielle Steel.

WHEN DOES BOOK BURNING ACTUALLY HELP FREE SPEECH?

The follies of censorship and its backlash

Book burning has a long, traumatic, hysterical, history. As long as books have been written, groups and governments have taken it upon themselves to limit the public's intake of material deemed unsavory. But the sad legacy of ritualized censorship has actually had some positive, if unintended, effects on the present state of free speech.

The earliest recorded occurrence of book burning took place in 213 BC in Ancient China, where the "burning of the books and burial of the scholars" saw the first emperor of China, Qin Shi Huang, try to "unify" the thoughts and opinions of his people by burning all histories except those written by his own historians. He not only burned books but also buried people, ordering more than 450 alchemists buried alive.

Hardy Retort

Copies of Thomas Hardy's novel *Jude the Obscure* (1895) were burned by the Bishop of Wakefield because of the novel's frank descriptions of Jude's sexual relationships. In a 1912 postscript, Hardy wrote, "After these verdicts from the press its next misfortune was to be burnt by a bishop—probably in his despair at not being able to burn me."

Throughout the centuries similar purgings have occurred when leaders or societies found ideas inconvenient; authority figures have targeted everything from agnostic Greek philosophy, Roman history books, Hebrew Bibles, Mayan sacred texts, and Christian writings.

Boccaccio's *Decameron*, with its raunchy tales about European life, is one of the earliest works of fiction (rather than religious or historical texts) to be burned. It was attacked during sermons in Italy during the fifteenth century and expurgated at various times during subsequent decades. In 1497, the Italian priest Girolamo

Savonarola ordered that the work, as well as anything by Ovid, be tossed into the flames. This event, in which pornography, cosmetics, and gaming tables were also incinerated, became known as the "bonfire of the vanities."

John Milton took up the issue after England passed the Licensing Order of 1643. In his pamphlet *Areopagitica* (1644), he lays out a case against censorship from a deeply religious perspective, urging that information and ideas should be disseminated freely if individuals are to make genuine choices (also major themes of *Paradise Lost*). He writes such bold defenses of free speech as, "who kills a man kills a reasonable creature, God's image; but he who destroys a good book, kills reason itself, kills the image of God, as it were, in the eye."

Did You Know?

Louisa May Alcott led an early charge to have *The Adventures of Huckleberry Finn* banned for its crude language, writing, "If Mr. Clemens cannot think of anything better to tell our pure-minded lads and lassies, he had better stop writing for them." After it was published in 1885, she worked to get it banned in her home state of Massachusetts. Naturally, sales quickly increased threefold.

Anthony Comstock, America's self-appointed censor-in-chief of the nineteenth century, called himself a "weeder in God's garden." He was a dedicated hunter of allegedly obscene works, beginning with his objections over the profanity used by his fellow soldiers whom he fought alongside in the Civil War. Serving as United States Postal Inspector, he was influential enough to push through the Comstock Act in 1873, which made it illegal to send "obscene, lewd, and/or lascivious" materials through the mail.

Comstock used his power to arrest those who distributed the offending material, which included journal articles about public scandals, information about contraceptives, sexually explicit marriage manuals, and even anatomy books. He eventually founded the New York Society for the Suppression of Vice (which actually features book burning on its seal), helping him to further his aims. Comstock's campaigns resulted in the destruction of fifteen tons of books and 284,000 pounds of plates for printing books. He boasted that his crusades had been responsible for 4,000 arrests and fifteen suicides (as a result of the humiliation felt by those caught with illegal material).

Did You Know?

When Comstock led the New York police commissioner to expurgate the promptbook before a performance of George Bernard Shaw's *Mrs. Warren's Profession* (1893) because of its discussion of prostitution, Shaw commented, "Comstockery is the world's standing joke at the expense of the United States. Europe likes to hear of such things. It confirms the deep-seated conviction of the Old World that America is a provincial place, a second-rate country-town civilization after all."

German writer Heinrich Heine wrote in his play *Almansor* (1821), "Where they burn books, so too will they in the end burn human beings." Heine's own works  were among those burned by the Nazis a century later among the many Jewish, anti-Nazi, and "degenerate" books burned in Germany in the 1930s and 1940s. The director of libraries in the German city of Essen determined some 18,000 works that disagreed with Nazi ideology, and which were incinerated.

The Nazi efforts culminated on May 10, 1933, an ominous day that presaged further state control of thought and language, as Nazi youth groups marched across the country playing music and singing joyous songs as they burned tens of thousands of books considered "un-German," including ones by Helen Keller, Thomas Mann, Sigmund Freud, H. G. Wells, and Albert Einstein. Dubbed a "bibliocaust" by the media, the burnings received local and international coverage and became emblematic of the dangers of censorship.

Voluntary Burning

Before he died, Franz Kafka wrote to his friend Max Brod to request that any diaries, manuscripts, letters, or sketches he left behind be burned. Brod refused, to the benefit of literature. Had he carried out the request, virtually all of Kafka's work, except for a handful of short stories he published while living, would have been destroyed.

The impact of Nazi book burnings was revealed for good when Senator Joseph McCarthy pressured President Dwight Eisenhower to have books by allegedly communist authors removed

from State Department libraries throughout Europe. While the president initially supported this purging, he turned on McCarthy in a speech at Dartmouth College, urging the students, "Don't join the book burners. Don't think you're going to conceal faults by concealing evidence that they ever existed. Don't be afraid to go in your library and read every book."

Did You Know?

Despite the title of Ray Bradbury's *Fahrenheit 451*, books actually burn at 450° Celsius. Bradbury felt "Fahrenheit" had a better sound when he devised the title of his novel about a book-burning dystopia. Intended as a critique of the issues he had with American society at the time, Bradbury wrote, "It follows then that when Hitler burned a book I felt it as keenly, please forgive me, as his killing a human, for in the long sum of history they are one and the same flesh."

A more recent series of book burnings took place in 1989, when a fatwa was placed on Salman Rushdie for writing *The Satanic Verses* (1988). Due to what was perceived as a negative depiction of the prophet Muhammad, Iran's Ayatollah Khomeini offered a bounty for Rushdie's execution. Violent demonstrations followed, including burnings of the book in the United Kingdom and the firebombing of bookstores in the U.K. and in Berkeley, California.

The book was banned in many countries with sizable Muslim populations, and Rushdie remained in hiding for years afterward. Not only Rushdie felt the force of this uproar. The Japanese translator of the work was stabbed to death, the Italian translator was stabbed but survived, and the Norwegian publisher was shot in the back.

Did You Know?

When the fatwa was placed on Rushdie, his friend and fellow author Ian McEwan provided him refuge in McEwan's Cotswolds cottage.

All the drama surrounding *The Satanic Verses* helped fuel huge sales. It had only middling sales when first published, but flew off the shelves after the fatwa, eventually becoming the sixth bestselling book of 1989.

These days, an effort to ban or burn a specific book or other type of work is likely to draw more protesters than supporters. The reactionary history of book burnings has turned many reflexively against the practice. This has been highlighted in recent years as some churches have protested that the *Harry Potter* series is "attached to the occult." Book burnings sponsored by a church in Alamogordo, New Mexico, in 2001, and one in Greenville, Michigan, in 2003 received massive publicity, most of it negative or mocking. The outsized coverage and protests of the events arguably did more to promote free speech and the *Harry Potter* books than to protect the youth from his wizardly ways.

WHAT DID CHILDREN READ BEFORE THERE WAS CHILDREN'S LITERATURE?

The battle for fun in kids' books, from hornbooks to Harry Potter

These days, kids have great options when looking for something to read. Whether a simple picture book, the latest *Twilight* installment, or a story about a wimpy kid trying to make it through middle school, there are children's books that speak to every taste. If there's an untapped demand, you can be sure a children's publisher will fill it and probably make a solid profit in the process. This wealth of options has come only after a long-fought battle between what children actually want to read and what adults think they should.

In ancient Greece and Rome, education was focused on molding children into well-rounded citizens in mind, body, and moral outlook. Boys attended schools where they were expected to memorize and recite passages from poems and plays (girls, lucky them, would occasionally learn to read and write at home when they were not cooking, cleaning, or mending). Teachers would dictate sections of Homer's *Iliad* or Virgil's *Aeneid* to students to copy into notebooks (books were much too expensive for each child to have). As they got older, children would read these works themselves, occasionally acting the roles. Always the goal was to educate and edify, not to entertain.

Did You Know?

For something lighter, kids could read *Aesop's Fables*, which were passed down for centuries and translated into numerous languages. Many are still popular today, including "The Boy Who Cried Wolf," "The Tortoise and the Hare," and "The Fox and the Grapes" (where the expression "sour grapes" originated).

As society's goals for educating children shifted, so did the books children were encouraged to read. In medieval times, the rise of new social segments including the feudal, royal, and mercantile classes led to new literatures aimed at each social class. Most children had started down their professional path by the time they were ten years old, and these new works aimed to instruct them in how to fulfill their duties—courtesy manuals for royals, apprenticeship guidelines for young merchants, and religious works for aspiring priests and nuns, for example.

Kids looking for a good story, however, could occasionally get their hands on recast versions of Thomas Malory's *Morte d'Arthur* (1486) or the narrative ballads of Robin Hood, targeted toward a younger audience. This entertaining literature met resistance from many who felt a child's education should have a more religious focus. William Tyndale, one of the principal translators of the King James Bible, spoke out against some of the burgeoning children's literature of the sixteenth century. He wrote, in *The Obedience of a Christian Man* (1528), that instead of reading scripture, children and laymen were being encouraged to:

Read Robin Hood and Bevis of Hampton, Hercules, Hector and Troilus with a thousand histories and fables of love and wantonness and of ribaldry as filthy as heart can think, to corrupt the minds of youth withal.

Tyndale's efforts were not in vain, and through the seventeenth century children's literature was dominated by Puritans working to cultivate the young into moral beings. John Bunyan's *Pilgrim's Progress* (1678) and James Janeway's *A Token for Children* (1671) were the must-read books for kids at the time (often in versions recast for younger readers, such as 1697's *Pilgrim's Progress in Poesie*).

Reading was seen as an extension of bible study. Prayer books and primers, sometimes called "hornbooks," combined basic alphabets with religious maxims, poetry, illustrations, and stories with a moral purpose. The books instructed children on their place in their family and society at large and touched on themes like sin and salvation.

William Shakespeare has a pun-filled riff on hornbooks in *Love's Labour Lost* (1598):

MOTH.	Yes, he teaches boys the hornbook. What is a, b, spelt backward with the horn on his head?
HOLOFERNES.	Ba, pueritia, with a horn added.
MOTH.	Ba, most silly sheep with a horn. You hear his learning.
HOLOFERNES.	Quis, quis, thou consonant?
MOTH.	The third of the five vowels, if you repeat them; or the fifth, if I.
HOLOFERNES.	I will repeat them: a, e,. —
MOTH.	The sheep; the other two concludes it: o, u.

Outside England and America, some interesting developments were taking place. Czech writer John Amos Comenius produced what is considered the first picture book, the *Orbis Sensualium Pictus* (*The Visible World of Pictures*), in 1658. It serves as a kind of child's encyclopedia, with chapters on botanics, zoology, religion, and "humans and their activities."

Around the same time, the French writer Charles Perrault was helping to establish the fairy tale. Perrault's stories were familiar to many throughout Europe, but had not been written down, including such enduring classics as "Little Red Riding Hood," "Sleeping Beauty," "Puss in Boots," and "Cinderella." He published a collection of eight of these stories in 1697, calling it *Stories or Tales from Times Past, with Morals* with the subtitle *Tales of Mother Goose* (the first such collection attributed to the figure, though "Mother Goose stories" may have been around for decades). These were translated into English in 1729.

Was Mother Goose a Witch?

Since Charles Perrault's collection, the character of Mother Goose has been depicted with some suspiciously witchlike traits. With pointed hat and nose and riding a goose through the air (instead of a broomstick perhaps?), her appearance, memorably depicted in the classic 1916 collection *The Real Mother Goose*, is believed to have pagan origins. The owls, frogs, cats, and of course geese that appear in the nursery rhymes and illustrations have been likened to the "familiars" associated with witches, and the rhymes as incantations.

Thanks in part to the influential writings of John Locke, it began to be accepted in England that education should not be rote learning in the classroom, but practical and entertaining. Bookseller John Newbery saw an opportunity in these development, and began publishing inexpensive works illustrated with woodcuts and engravings, marketing them as not only valuable for a child's development but also fun to read.

The first of these, *A Little Pretty Pocket-Book* (1744), is considered the first children's book in England. Each one of his subsequent books, including the enormously popular *The History of Little Goody Two-Shoes* (1765), all featured advertisements for his other books within the stories themselves and sold at a steady clip. Newbery showed how marketable children's books could be, and others soon followed his lead.

Quick Quote

"You have to write the book that wants to be written. And if the book will be too difficult for grown-ups, then you write it for children."
—Madeleine L'Engle, author of *A Wrinkle in Time* (1962)

Grimm's *Fairy Tales* (1823), James Orchard Halliwell-Phillipp's nursery rhymes, and Hans Christian Andersen's *Fairy Tales* (translated to English in 1846) found immense popularity chiefly for their entertainment value. The growing demand for amusement, not morality, was made clear when George Cruikshank attempted to rewrite traditional fairy tales as lessons on the evil of alcohol consumption, with none other than Charles Dickens calling him out on his moralizing. In his 1853 essay "Frauds on the Fairies," Dickens writes:

> Now, it makes not the least difference to our objection whether we agree or disagree with our worthy friend, Mr. Cruikshank, in the opinions he interpolates upon

an old fairy story. Whether good or bad in themselves, they are, in that relation, like the famous definition of a weed; a thing growing up in a wrong place.

Dickens was not alone in his opinions, as evidenced by William Thackeray's *The Rose and the Ring* (1855) and Charles Kingsley's *The Water Babies* (1863), which focused first on fantastical descriptions and characters, and secondarily on offering a lesson. Edward Lear's *Book of Nonsense* (1846), abandoned meaning altogether, aiming to please young ears with the sound of words while letting children make up their own definitions. The pinnacle of these surrealistic kids' books came with Lewis Carroll's *Alice's Adventures in Wonderland* (1865), a book offering deranged fantasy and word games, with hardly a moral lesson in sight. It was an immediate success with both adults and children.

Name Games

- J. M. Barrie popularized, and some say actually invented, the name "Wendy." Before his play *Peter Pan* and novel *Peter and Wendy* were published in the early twentieth century, the name was virtually unheard of. Barrie is thought to have gotten it from the daughter of his friend, who mispronounced her "R"s when she said, "fwiendy-wendy."
- "Pinocchio" means "pine nut" in Italian.
- "Cinderella" is derived from the fact that the character sits in cinder and ashes before escaping her destitute surroundings. Earlier versions and translations of the tale called her, among other names, "Aschenputtel" and "The Hearth Cat."

Through the early twentieth century, children's literature continued to diversify, with writers like A. A. Milne, J. M. Barrie and L. Frank Baum (initials were all the rage at this time) creating entire franchises around their memorable characters, including book series, stage plays, and merchandise. Beatrix Potter's best-selling *The Tale of Peter Rabbit* (1902) spawned not only twenty-three books but also Peter Rabbit games, wallpaper, stationary, stuffed toys, and figurines shortly after the book was published. Besides making these authors and their publishers rich, these brand extensions further established children's literature as a true entertainment industry, setting the stage for the films and television spin-offs that would follow in later decades.

Who Needs English?

Lewis Carroll, Beatrix Potter, and Enid Blyton (author of the hugely popular *Noddy* books and *Famous Five* series) top the children's bestsellers in English, but their sales hardly compare to the 160 million Tintin books that Belgian Georges Remi (Hergé) has sold, or the quarter billion in sales of the French René Goscinny and Albert Uderzo's Asterix books. Despite their major success in various translations throughout the globe (and their largely illustrated content), neither have done particularly well in Britain or the United States.

As children's literature has matured, so to speak, meeting the demands for a variety of tastes, the line between adult and young adult fiction has become increasingly thin. Writers such as J. R. R. Tolkien, C. S. Lewis, and Roald Dahl have remained relevant even as readers move on to more adult works.

More recently, authors like Philip Pullman, J. K. Rowling, and Stephenie Meyer have commanded the bestseller lists, with adults as likely as children to pick up their latest books (or view the latest film based on them). In 2001, *The New York Times* created a "Children's Books" bestseller list because the first three *Harry Potter* books had monopolized the top positions of the adult list for over a year. After centuries of kids having to read like grownups, it seems like adults are now choosing to read like kids.

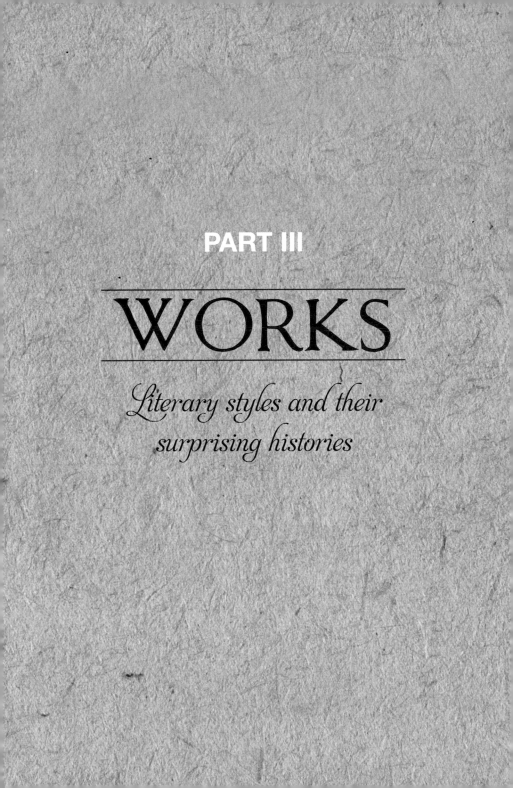

PART III

WORKS

*Literary styles and their
surprising histories*

WHO ELEVATED INSULTS TO AN ART FORM?

When authors attack
(with invective and satire)

People have surely been hurling insults at one another since we were able to grunt, but some notable figures in the history of literature took denunciation to glorious levels. Whether criticizing individuals, institutions, or society at large, poets and writers from Juvenal to Jonathan Swift helped turn vicious take-downs into a laudable art form.

The history of insults began in classical time with two men of very different dispositions—one cruel, one kind. The Roman poet Juvenal was one nasty dude. He penned ferocious attacks on the vices and many offenses of the Roman lifestyle, particularly those perpetrated by the rich and female. His masterworks are the *Satires*, a series of sixteen lengthy poems written in the late first century. The poems denounce Roman pretensions and greed and even the fashion choices of one judge Juvenal particularly disliked:

> However guilty, [criminals] would never wear such a gown as yours. "O but," you say, "these July days are so sweltering!" Then why not plead without clothes? Such madness would be less disgraceful . . . What would you not exclaim if you saw a judge dressed like that?

Ouch. The other great ancient insulter was Horace, less strident than Juvenal and generally more playful in his satires (and likely more frequently invited to ancient Roman parties). His works examine the pursuit of a happy and satisfied life; he observes that superstition is for fools and that because human sexual urges are easily satisfied, running after married women is silly.

Samuel Johnson defined satire as "a poem in which wickedness or folly is censured." Horace's kinder, gentler satire has been an inspiration to many works that aim an amused smile at "folly," from Jonathan Swift's *Gulliver's Travels* (1726) to C. S. Lewis's *The Screwtape Letters* (1942), in which a senior demon counsels a less experienced tempter in the failings of human beings. Those looking to make a harsher indictment of "wickedness," channel Juvenal, and the influence of the poet's acid tongue can be seen in works like Swift's "A Modest Proposal" (1729) and George Orwell's *Nineteen Eighty-Four* (1949).

Satire flourished during the Renaissance and the seventeenth century. Ben Jonson's "humour" plays, in which characters are

dominated by a specific emotion, gently mocked various types of foolish behavior and created something of a trend in the period.

Shakespeare could truly brandish an insult. In works such as *Troilus and Cressida* (1602), *King Lear* (1608), and *The Tempest* (1623), the Bard lets the invectives fly, like this one from *Lear:*

> A knave, a rascal, an eater of broken meats; a base, proud, shallow, beggarly, three-suited, hundred-pound, filthy worsted-stocking knave; a lily-livered, action-taking, whoreson, glass-gazing, super-serviceable, finical rogue; one-trunk-inheriting slave; one that wouldst be a bawd in way of good service, and art nothing but the composition of a knave, beggar, coward, pander, and the son and heir to a mongrel bitch: one whom I will beat into clamorous whining if thou deni'st the least syllable of thy addition.

Shakespeare's insults were downright kind when compared to some of the brutally satiric works released by contemporaries like Joseph Hall and Thomas Middleton during the final years of Elizabeth's reign (a period of general national disillusionment). These works irked the powers that be, since they attacked England's established institutions, eventually leading to a "Bishops' Ban" in 1599, prohibiting the printing of satires.

This silenced critical writings for a while, but the Age of Enlightenment, with its love of rationality, order, and the wisdom of the ancients, helped usher in the golden age of satire. Writers like John Dryden, Swift, and Alexander Pope used their poems and stories to poke fun at the excesses they saw in individuals and institutions around them.

A Club of Jokers

While they dedicated many couplets to criticizing their fellow men, the great neoclassical (early eighteenth century, also know as the Augustan Age because of its emulation of classical works and the era. of Caesar Augustan) satirists were quite chummy with each other. Pope, Swift, John Gay, Thomas Parnell, and several other writers went so far as to form the Scriblerus Club, which met regularly to chat and needle "all the false tastes in learning." They even collaborated on the work *Memoirs of Martinus Scriblerus* (1741).

Satire would bring writers together in later periods as well, most notably the Algonquin Round Table of New York writers in the 1920s. The writers and wits in the group included Dorothy Parker, Robert Benchley, and *New Yorker* editor Harold Ross, although their daily lunches at the Algonquin Hotel were spent directing wisecracks and practical jokes at each other as much as at broader cultural targets.

In "An Essay Upon Satire" (1679), Dryden provides a manifesto for mockery for his age, explaining that:

Satire has always shone among the rest,
And is the boldest way, if not the best,
To tell men freely of their foulest faults;
To laugh at their vain deeds, and vainer thoughts.

But the poet acknowledges at the end of the work that "I, who so wise and humble seem to be, / Now my own vanity and pride can't see."

Pope's *The Rape of the Lock* (1717) humorously turns a petty argument into a mock epic in which the theft of the heroine's lock of hair is treated on the scale of Helen's abduction from Troy in

The Iliad. In Dryden's poem *Mac Flecknoe* (1682), he takes aim at fellow poet Thomas Shadwell by presenting him as the heir to the kingdom of poetic mediocrity.

Unlike the Elizabethan satirists before them, the writers in the Augustan age viewed their work as a way to maintain the moral order by calling out the excesses of their fellow men, rather than using their pen to lob criticisms at the order itself. These works were meant to skewer their targets with Horatian meticulousness, rather than bludgeon them with the misanthropy of Juvenal, which was simply not their style.

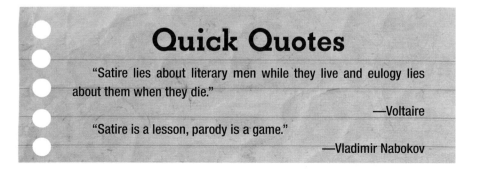

Satire continued to thrive throughout the nineteenth century, particularly with the publication of satiric magazines like *Punch* and *Fun*, and into the twentieth century in works as wide-ranging as Sinclair Lewis's *Babbitt* (1922), poking fun at the vacuity of American culture, to Anthony Burgess's *A Clockwork Orange* (1962), with its "ultra-violent" Juvenalian exaggeration of the dangers of totalitarian rule. Satire may not hold the honored place in the literary world that it did during the neoclassical era, but its popularity has endured,

Quick Quotes

"Satire lies about literary men while they live and eulogy lies about them when they die."

—Voltaire

"Satire is a lesson, parody is a game."

—Vladimir Nabokov

from *The Onion* newspaper to *The Daily Show*. As long as people and institutions continue to do foolish things, satire will likely remain an enduring art.

Poison Pens

While writers of satire could lay out some cruel condemnations of social ills and human failure in their works, some of the best zingers in literature come from writers bashing fellow writers. Some choice words:

William Faulkner on Mark Twain: "A hack writer who would not have been considered fourth rate in Europe, who tricked out a few of the old proven 'sure-fire' literary skeletons with sufficient local color to intrigue the superficial and the lazy."

Henry James on Edgar Allan Poe: "An enthusiasm for Poe is the mark of a decidedly primitive stage of reflection."

Virginia Woolf on James Joyce: "[*Ulysses* is] the work of a queasy undergraduate scratching his pimples."

D.H. Lawrence on Herman Melville: "Nobody can be more clownish, more clumsy and sententiously in bad taste, than Herman Melville, even in a great book like *Moby-Dick*.... There's something false about it. And that's Melville. Oh dear, when the solemn ass brays! brays! brays!"

George Bernard Shaw on William Shakespeare: "The intensity of my imapatience with him occasionally reaches such a pitch, that it would positively be a relief to me to dig him up and throw stones at him, knowing as I do how incapable he and his worshippers are of understanding any less obvious form of indignity."

Gore Vidal on Truman Capote: "He's a full-fledged housewife from Kansas with all the prejudices."

Elizebeth Bishop on J.D. Salinger's *The Catcher in the Rye:* "I HATED the Salinger story. It took me days to go through it, gingerly, a page at a time, and blushing with embarrassment for him every ridiculous sentence of the way. How can they let him do it?"

WHAT MAKES SOMETHING ODE-WORTHY?

The surprising range of the lyrical poem

When a poet wants to say something of high emotion and praise, he or she is very likely to reach for the ode. This stately form of poetry, with its elaborate stanza structure and lofty language, has been used for centuries to honor historical victories and joyous events. It can also be used to praise peculiar inanimate objects or, perhaps, anything. The ode is one of the loftiest kinds of poems, but there is little limit to what it can be, and has been, dedicated to.

For example, William Collins published an "Ode to Fear" in 1747 ("Who, Fear, this ghastly train can see, / And look not madly wild like thee?") and one of W. H. Auden's great ones is "In Praise of Limestone" ("This land is not the sweet home that it looks, / Nor its peace the historical calm of a site / Where something was settled once and for all"), published in 1948.

Odes are generally categorized into two main groups: public and private. The public odes have been used for ceremonial occasions like significant birthdays, funerals, and celebrations. Tennyson's "Ode on the Death of the Duke of Wellington" (1852) is a good example of public odes. The godfather of this type of ode is considered to be Pindar, who honored victors of Greek games and other public celebration, usually accompanied by music and dancing ("ode" is actually Greek for "song"). For something to be a "Pindaric ode" usually requires stanzas in a pattern of three—the strophe, antistrophe, and epode.

The Romans were a bit more introspective in their odes, and Horace remains the dominant ode-maker of the Romans (the same man who pioneered satire, as discussed in the previous chapter), developing a more meditative style, which celebrated intense, personal experiences, friendships, and the like. The Romantics loved the private odes for these reasons. Each stanza of a formal Horatian ode has the same stanza and metrical pattern.

Edmund Spenser raised the ode to epic heights with "Epithalamion" (1595), a 433-line wedding poem written for his bride Elizabeth Boyle. The twenty-four stanzas can be seen as corresponding to the twenty-four hours of the wedding day (not a bad wedding gift). He doubled down the next year with "Prothalamion" (1596), a poem written for the twin marriages of the daughters of the Earl of Worcester, who are referred to as "two swans of goodly hue."

Many Other Celebrated Poets Wrote Epithalamions, Including:

- Theocritus → Greek poet celebrated Menelaus and Helen's marriage.
- Catullus → Roman poet wrote an ode to the marriage of Thetis and Peleus.
- John Donne → "Epithalamion Made at Lincoln's Inn" ends every stanza with "Today put on perfection, and a woman's name."
- Sir John Suckling → "A Ballad Upon a Wedding" demystifies marriage with a comic, plainspoken style.
- Gerard Manley Hopkins → Ostensibly about the marriage of unnamed bride and bridegroom, but spends a lot of time discussing young boys bathing.
- e.e. cummings → Heavy on the erotic language, from "quivering continual thighs" to "the warm long flower of unchastity."

Ben Jonson contributed his own epithalamion, but is perhaps more notable for being the first to bring the Pindaric style to English, with his "Ode to Sir Lucius Cary and Sir H. Morison" (1629).

While Milton did not describe any of his poems as odes, a few, such as his formally complex "On the Morning of Christ's Nativity" (1645), are widely seen as fulfilling all the requirements of an ode in the Pindaric style. He certainly spoke in a high-minded way, writing to his friend Charles Diodati, "I sing to the peace-bringing God descended from heaven, and the blessed generations covenanted in the sacred books . . . I sing the starry axis and the singing hosts in the sky, and of the gods suddenly destroyed in their own shrines." One of his earliest poems, "On the Death of a Fair Infant Dying of a Cough" (1626), was essentially an ode written after his sister Anne Phillips miscarried.

Andrew Marvell wrote his "An Horatian Ode upon Cromwell's Return from Ireland" (1650), to celebrate Cromwell coming back to England after his subjugation of Ireland, and looks forward to his campaign against the Scots. Abraham Cowley followed the Pindaric public tone, but dropped the involved metrical structure and liberally altered the stanzas and lines. John Dryden had many of the big odes during the period, though, including "Threnodia Augustalis" (1685), "Ode to the Memory of Mrs Anne Killigrew" (1686), "Song for St Cecilia's Day" (1687), and "Alexander's Feast" (1697).

In the eighteenth century Anne Finch, Countess of Winchilsea wrote a Pindaric poem on "The Spleen," and Alexander Pope composed the Horatian "Ode on Solitude" (written when he was twelve years old) and the Pindaric "Ode for Music on St Cecilia's Day."

Some of the more interesting odes composed during this time include Collins's "Ode to Evening," "Ode to Simplicity," "Ode to Fear," "Ode to Mercy," and "Ode on the Poetical Character." Gray provided "Ode on Spring," "Ode on a Distant Prospect of Eton College," "Ode on Adversity," and "Ode on the Death of a Favorite Cat, Drowned in a Tub of Gold Fishes," which details a curious tabby's tragic slip as she tries to get lunch out of the goldfish bowl:

> Presumptuous Maid! with looks intent
> Again she stretch'd, again she bent,
> Nor knew the gulph between;
> (Malignant Fate sat by, and smil'd.)
> The slippery verge her feet beguil'd;
> She tumbled headlong in.

Did You Know?

The "Favorite Cat" of the poem was that of Gray's friend the gothic novelist Horace Walpole, whose cat actually did die in a china vase.

The ode really came into its own during the Romantic era. Its meditative and lyrical possibilities dovetailed nicely with the Romantics' appreciation for nature and self-exploration. The big odes of this time include Coleridge's "France" and "Dejection:

An Ode," Wordsworth's "Ode on Intimations of Immortality" and "Ode to Duty," as well as Percy Bysshe Shelley's "Ode to the West Wind" (1820). Of course, the master of the ode was Keats, with the string of six gems written in a little over half a year (when the poet was a mere twenty-four years old): "On a Grecian Urn," "To a Nightingale," "To Autumn'" "On Melancholy," "On Indolence," and "To Psyche."

Romantic poets including Keats, Shelley, and Coleridge (and later poets like Swinburne and Hopkins) were much looser about the form and subject matter of odes than its classical counterparts. They also did not shy away from dedicating them to unhappy situations as often as to upbeat ones. Coleridge's "Dejection: An Ode" sees nature not as some benevolent force, as Wordsworth does, but claims that our own imagination assigns it those feelings. Keats's "On Melancholy" and "On Indolence" are less than upbeat.

Did You Know?

Coleridge, unhappily married, originally addressed *Dejection: An Ode* to Sara Hutchinson, with whom he was in love. In a later version he changes this to his friend, "O Wordsworth," only to bring Sara back (though this time anonymously referred to as "O Lady") in the final published text.

Few odes have been able to touch these massive works since, but Tennyson's "Ode on the Death of the Duke of Willington" (1852) and Allen Tate's "Ode to the Confederate Dead," as well as Auden's "In Praise of Limestone," have been hailed for their quality and inventiveness.

As far as quirkiness, it may be hard to touch the great Spanish-language poet Pablo Neruda, who published a collection of *Odes to Common Things* that gives the lyric treatment to everything from tomatoes, a large tuna in the market, and scissors. Though he is not quite as formal and complex as the ode usually calls for, it's easy to forgive lines like "two immense blackbirds, / two cannons, / my feet were honored in this way / by these heavenly socks," in "Ode to My Socks."

WHEN DID LITERATURE FINALLY GET SEXY?

How Shakespeare and others slipped sex into their works

Philip Larkin famously begins his poem "Annus Mirabilis" (1967) with the lines, "Sexual intercourse began / In nineteen sixty-three / (which was rather late for me)." While sexual intercourse obviously began well before the 1960s, Larkin's words point to the often secretive existence that sex has had in literature throughout the centuries. While idealized notions of love are the foundation for a vast range of literary works, the physical consummation of these emotions has generally been addressed in coded language while explicit discussions of sex have caused scandal.

Erotic writing about sex and sexual love can be traced back to ancient Greece and Rome, when writing shifted from epic stories of heroes and gods to choral songs that described everyday life— which for poets, such as ancient Greek writer Sappho, included sensual descriptions of sex.

Did You Know?

Sappho often wrote about the beauty of women, and her female speakers expressed love and infatuation for members of their own sex, which explains why the word "sapphic" derives from her name and "lesbian" derives from Lesbos, the Greek island where Sappho was born.

One of the earliest depictions of sex in literature is Boccaccio's *Decameron* (1353), which features subtly raunchy tales of love and coded references like "making the nightingale sing" and "riding the horse" in its 100 novellas. This was followed by Chaucer's *Troilus and Criseyde* (c. 1385), which follows the progress of a love affair between the two characters, describing their pursuit of courtly love in high-minded, though erotically charged terms.

While *Troilus and Criseyde* elevated love to divine heights, Chaucer's *Canterbury Tales* provides some early examples of sex used for laughs. The collection includes fabliaux (short, bawdy poems) such as *The Miller's Tale,* with its protagonist's elaborate scheme to cuckold his landlord, and *The Reeve's Tale*, in which two students get revenge on a dishonest miller by bedding his daughter and wife. Chaucer's contrasting approaches to sex, both highbrow and lowbrow, set the pattern for centuries to come.

The next landmark of erotic literature is Christopher Marlowe's *Hero and Leander* (1598). Rather than building to a climax of marriage (as was typical of works in this period), the poem ramps up to a monumental sex scene. After swimming across the strait of Hellespont and convincing Neptune not to drag him to the bottom of the sea, Leander arrives at Hero's door stark naked and ready for love. With the sexual tension at a peak, Hero's attempts to "defend her fort" are no match for Leander's advances:

Yet there with Sisyphus he toiled in vain,
Till gentle parley did the truce obtain.
Wherein Leander on her quivering breast,
Breathless spoke something, and sighed out the rest.

While much of Shakespeare's legacy rests on his treatment of romantic love, he delved into more explicit eroticism in his poetry. *Venus and Adonis* (1593) includes what may be the most graphic description of sex in Shakespeare, as Venus takes Adonis' hand and, "Backward she push'd him, as she would be thrust," and soon enough, "was she along as he was down, Each leaning on their elbows and their hips." Racy stuff.

Shakespeare was also of course a master of sexual puns and dirty jokes. Entire books compiling his innuendos have been written, but a few favorites include:

- "It must be an answer of most monstrous size that must fit all demands."—The Countess to Lavatch in *All's Well That Ends Well,* whose "bountiful answer . . . fits all questions," or serves the sexual needs of all.
- "By my life, this is my lady's hand. These be her very c's, her u's, and her t's, and thus makes she her great p's."
- "With thou, whose will is large and spacious, / Not once vouchsafe to hide my will in thine?"—in Sonnet 135, the Bard uses his own first name to refer to the sexual organs of himself and his would-be lover.

Sex took a more cerebral turn with metaphysical poets like John Donne and Andrew Marvell, who crafted elaborate metaphors, known as metaphysical conceits, using their verses as tools of seduction. Donne turns the title creature of "The Flea" (1633) into a stand-in for sexual intercourse as it "sucks" the speaker and his would-be lover and "swells with one blood." Pointing out that neither of the two are any weaker for this loss of bodily fluid, the speaker slyly argues that "Just so much honour, when thou yield'st to me, / Will waste, as this flea's death took life from thee." In "Elegy XIX: To His Mistress Going to Bed" (1633), Donne compares fondling his love to the exploration of America.

Marvell's "To His Coy Mistress" (1681) is perhaps the masterpiece of the metaphysical seduction poem, complete with references to "vegetable love" and an urging to "Roll all our strength and / Our sweetness into one ball, / And tear our pleasures with rough strife."

Did You Know?

John Donne was the first writer to use the word "sex" in its present sense in his poem "The Primrose" (1631)

For should my true-love less than woman be,
She were scarce anything; and then, should she
Be more than woman, she would get above
All thought of sex, and think to move
My heart to study her, and not to love.

When England's theaters reopened in 1660 after the monarchy was restored under Charles II, the gates of raunchiness were yanked open wider. The Restoration comedies of the late seventeenth century took sex talk back to its fabliau roots, with rakish behavior and debauchery as central to works like

William Wycherley's *The Country Wife* (1675), George Etherege's *The Man of Mode* (1676), and Aphra Behn's *The Rover* (1677)—Behn, the first woman playwright, proved that bawdy talk was not just a man's game.

The Country Wife is loaded with sex so thinly disguised it would make Shakespeare blush. The lead character, suggestively named Horner, feigns impotence, which allows him to bed the wives of his comrades right under their noses (and just out of the audience's view). The famous "china scene" features an extended double entendre in which, after making love with one woman, another accosts Horner and demands she, "have some china too." Horner responds, "Do not take it ill, I cannot make china for you all."

As much fun as the Restoration period was for theater fans, it pushed the envelope a bit too far for some. Theater critic Jeremy Collier's *A Short View of the Immorality and Profaneness of the English Stage* (1698) asserts that "nothing has gone farther in debauching the age than the stage poets, and play-house." His essay led to a pamphlet war among critics and playwrights, which prompted theaters to dial down the crude humor and restored a sense of propriety for decades to come.

Did You Know?

When two ladies complimented Dr. Samuel Johnson for omitting naughty words from his *Dictionary*, the writer responded, "What! My dears! Then you have been looking for them?"

Once the sex talk had entered the literary conversation, it was hard to silence it. John Cleland's *Fanny Hill, or, Memoirs of a Woman of Pleasure* (1749), which graphically chronicles the exploits and adventures of a young prostitute, caused a major scandal as the first erotic novel, and the publication of the second installment led to the prompt arrest of both Cleland and his publishers. The battle between smut-peddlers and the strait-laced would continue for the next two centuries, with the former gaining ground after every uproar.

The Romantics flirted with eroticism, but were more preoccupied with imagination and fantasy than discussing the act itself (Lord Byron was better known for his real-life sexual adventures than any descriptive poetry). This would shift into more frank treatments of sex, followed by predictable scandal, in the mid-nineteenth century.

In France, the sexual descriptions in Gustave Flaubert's *Madame Bovary* caused an outcry when it was serialized in *La Revue de Paris* in 1856, eventually going to trial. It won acquittal and instantly became a bestseller. In America, Walt Whitman sang the praises of sex in raw and graphic terms throughout his landmark *Leaves of Grass* (1855); critics were offended, and the publisher considered holding up the publication of the second edition. The depictions of homoerotic love in particular did not sit well with some reviewers, with one suggesting Whitman was guilty of "that horrible sin not to be mentioned among Christians."

Did You Know?

Although Whitman was often explicit in his poetry, he was a bit guarded in his own diary. When writing about his longtime lover—Irish bus conductor Peter Doyle—he would refer to him as "16.4," as "P" is the sixteenth letter in the alphabet and "D" is the fourth.

A victory for graphic sex in literature came in 1959, when an effort to ban D. H. Lawrence's *Lady Chatterley's Lover,* Henry Miller's *Tropic of Cancer*, and *Fanny Hill* in America was overturned in court. Both Miller's and Lawrence's books were lauded by literary critics when finally published and were smash hits with audiences eager to see what was so scandalous.

After this high-profile victory for explicit literature, efforts at censorship became increasingly tricky, and sex became less taboo. In the second half of the twentieth century, celebrated authors like Philip Roth and John Updike wrote explicit accounts of the male's sexual experience with comparatively little sensation from the public, while nonfiction works like Alex Comfort's *The Joy of Sex* (1972), Nancy Friday's *My Secret Garden* (1973), and Erica Jong's autobiographical novel *Fear of Flying* (1973) became bestsellers. As Larkin said: sexual intercourse had arrived—and not a moment too soon.

Did You Know?

For reasons probably only known to her, Gertrude Stein referred to orgasms as "cows." When she writes, "a wife has a cow," or about "making a cow come out," Stein is not talking about farming.

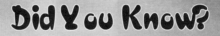

WHY IS SATAN THE GREATEST BAD GUY EVER?

Literary villains and why we love them

Heroes get the girl, but villains win the reader. We may hiss at the bad guy when he pops into the story to wreak his (or her) havoc, but the villain is most likely to stick with us long after we've closed the book. Despite the important role they play in many great works, baddies have not always been a fixture of great literature.

Monsters are present throughout classical as well as early English works, from the intimidating Cyclops in the *Odyssey* to the towering Green Knight with a removable head in *Sir Gawain and the Green Knight*, villains as we traditionally understand them actually originated in medieval English plays.

Did You Know?

The word "villain" actually comes from the Anglo-French term *villein*, which means "farmhand." The phrase referred to those who were bound to the land and were therefore of a less than genteel status. This came to simply mean "not chivalrous" and a term of abuse that implied the corrupt character of rapists and criminals, eventually acquiring its modern meaning.

Shakespeare refers to the original meaning of the word in *As You Like It*, when he writes, "I am no villain; I am the youngest son of Sir Rowland de Boys; he was my father, and he is thrice a villain that says such a father begot villains."

Early plays were mystery and morality dramas, based on biblical stories that delivered a poignant Christian message to audiences. Angels and devils (and sometimes God and Satan) were integral parts of this storytelling. The devil entered the drama and tried to lure the protagonist into sin, while the angels urged him to resist, and usually won out, bringing the play to a happy close.

The devils were easily the most entertaining part of these otherwise stodgy moral lessons. They were slapstick clowns telling bawdy jokes, getting chased around the stage, and falling down. It should be no surprise that these satanic troublemakers remained a staple of medieval theater through the seventeenth century—long after the angels ceased to play key roles. It would seem the angels' victories were short-lived.

Over the decades, devils evolved (or devolved, depending on your perspective), becoming more human, while some of the sketchy human characters became more diabolical, bringing us to the first traditional villains in literature—the evildoers of Elizabethan and Jacobean tragedy.

These diabolized humans include such charming characters as D'Amville in Cyril Tourneur's *The Atheist's Tragedy* (1611), who has his brother killed and tries to do the same to his nephew before going insane and, in an exhibition of considerable will, killing himself with an ax. There's Ferdinand from John Webster's *The Duchess of Malfi* (1623), whose creepy attraction to his twin sister drives him to have her executed in a jealous rage. Afterward, he goes insane and runs around exhuming graves (derangement was apparently in vogue at the time).

Did You Know?

If there was one individual who can be credited with spawning modern villainy, it was Niccolò Machiavelli. The philosopher, diplomat, and playwright offered cutthroat advice to politicians and royalty in his famous treatise *The Prince,* first published in 1532. Tossing humanistic idealism out the window in favor of pure self-interested ambition, he provided an outlook equally seductive and abhorrent to right-thinking Renaissance readers at the time—and a compellingly amoral example that remains an inspiration to writers to this day.

The ghost of Machiavelli cameos in Christopher Marlowe's play *The Jew of Malta* (1592). As a character, he introduces the story of a man who lost his fortune and poisoned his own daughter and an entire nunnery before dying at the hands of the Turkish army.

Unlike the devils, these human miscreants weren't born bad; they were often wronged early in the story, which led them to villainy. This style of "revenge tragedy" was huge during this time, sparked by the plays of the Roman poet Seneca, whose *Ten Tragedies* were translated into English between 1559 and 1581.

Leave it to William Shakespeare to add intriguing complexity to these sinister rogues. His plays feature some of the most brilliant villains literature had ever seen, both in their calculating evil and their recognizable humanity. Hamlet's duplicitous uncle Claudius—or as Hamlet calls him, "Remorseless, treacherous, lecherous, kindless villain!"—is a calculating, ambitious politician, driven by his sexual appetites and his lust for power, but who also shows signs of deep guilt and human feeling. The ambitious Lady Macbeth is certainly remorseless, yet is suicidally conflicted about her crimes. Of course, figures like the calculating Iago, ambitious Richard III, and just plain nasty Aaron the Moor may be a bit harder to relate to, but are no less compelling as villains.

Killer Lines

Villains, particularly those in Shakespeare, have all the best lines— here are some memorably sinister ones:

"If one good deed in all my life I did, I do repent it from my very soul."

—Aaron the Moor, *Titus Andronicus*

"I have given suck, and know
How tender 'tis to love the babe that milks me:
I would, while it was smiling in my face,
Have pluck'd my nipple from his boneless gums,
And dash'd the brains out, had I so sworn as you."

—Lady Macbeth, *Macbeth*

"One does not establish a dictatorship in order to safeguard a revolution; one makes the revolution in order to establish the dictatorship."

—O'Brien, *1984*

> "It would have been better for all of you, lady, if you hadn't of reckernized me."
>
> —The Misfit, "A Good Man is Hard to Find"
>
> "War was always here. Before man was, war waited for him. The ultimate trade awaiting its ultimate practitioner . . . War is god."
>
> —Judge Holden, *Blood Meridian*
>
> "I'm utterly insane."
>
> —Patrick Bateman, *American Psycho*

The greatest villain in all of literature may very well be Milton's portrayal of Satan in *Paradise Lost* (1667). As Satan, he is, of course, irredeemably evil; and yet, Milton humanizes him. Beginning as a regal lord of the underworld, Satan transforms over the course of the epic into a lowly, vicious snake. Satan combines the evil (and occasional silliness) of the early devils as well as the more complex, seductive, and even sympathetic quality of the revenge tragedy villains, though in his case he's out for vengeance against all of humanity. In this way, he combines all the basic characteristics of the villains who preceded him over the previous three hundred years, tragically declaring, "Farewell Remorse: all Good to me is lost; / Evil be thou my Good."

The villain becomes much less common for decades after *Paradise Lost* (perhaps after Milton, writers knew they had best sit it out for a century), but returns with a vengeance in nineteenth-century melodrama. In these works, the villain reverts back into a satanic and slightly idiotic character to be hissed at and booed—this is when black hats, capes, and curly mustaches became the standard uniform.

This era also saw the rise of the far more complicated gothic villains. Often these could be the scary creeps that were typical in the revenge tragedies of earlier eras (dukes and monks bent on ruining the lives of the innocent heroines), but then there are those much more ambiguous figures who dance between being enemy and lover.

For example, there's Heathcliff in Emily Brontë's *Wuthering Heights* (1847), who plays the romantic lead through the first volume, only to lose the girl and turn into a bitter villain bent on revenge in the second volume. Edward Rochester in Charlotte Brontë's *Jane Eyre,* published the same year, does something of the opposite, transforming from an unfriendly character with a shady history into the heroic savior. They are what critic Deborah Lutz describes as "dangerous lovers" who both attract and repulse while keeping the reader eagerly flipping pages.

Did You Know?

Professor Moriarty, Sherlock Holmes's brilliant nemesis, and reputedly the first "supervillain" in literature, is based on two very different real-life sources. The first is Adam Worth, a German American criminal mastermind. Dubbed "the Napoleon of crime" by Scotland Yard, he was known as one of the greatest thieves of the nineteenth century. Second was the famous (and law-abiding) American astronomer Simon Newcomb. The real-life counterpart shared much with Moriarty, including a genius for mathematics, published papers on the binomial theorem (published when very young), and later work on the orbits of asteroids. Moriarity is truly an amalgam of good and evil influences.

These gothic villains in many ways typify the reader's own "love to hate" relationships with literature's great scoundrels. As authors continued to create wonderfully awful characters, from Count Dracula to Lord Voldemort, these villains continued to frighten and intrigue. Even while Voldemort claims the mantle of "the most powerful Dark Wizard who ever lived," it's hard not to think that for all his intimidation tactics, he's still got nothing on Milton's Satan.

WHY DID ROMANTICS LOVE TERROR (AND NOT HORROR)?

Gothic fiction and ghost stories

While scary stories go back to ancient folktales, and perhaps earlier, in the Romantic period, stories meant to terrify really took off. Part of this had to do with the Augustan period that preceded the Romantic era: While writers of the early eighteenth century embraced classicism and rationality, the Romantics turned to nature and the imagination for inspiration and freedom from their too-orderly surroundings. The Romantic era, which kicked off roughly around the middle of the eighteenth century, embraced strong emotions and sought out the sublime and a creative energy that went beyond the earthly and everyday. As it welcomed these supernatural elements, Romanticism also ushered in the heyday of the spooky. Gothic fiction, the genre that combined horror and romance and thrived for the following century, was the main by-product of these trends.

The genre evolved in the eighteenth century, beginning with Horace Walpole's *The Castle of Otranto* (1764), with its evil lord and mysterious and seemingly supernatural events and settings. While neoclassical style and architecture was all about orderliness and proportion, gothic style was about power, awe, and magnitude, and it was a hit with readers.

The genre really hit its stride with Ann Radcliffe, whose novels *The Romance of the Forest* (1791), *Mysteries of Udolpho* (1794), and *The Italian* (1797) made the gothic more palatable for a mass audience. By incorporating a more virtuous heroine and explaining the supernatural events taking place at the end of the story, it offered a compelling read with a moral message. The book was a smash and opened the floodgates to a torrent of other Gothic works, with twenty to thirty titles produced each year.

Radcliffe aimed to elicit terror from her readers but held back on horrific details, which proved an effective combination. In her essay, "On the Supernatural in Poetry," the author explains why she makes this choice:

> Terror and Horror are so far opposite, that the first expands the soul and awakens the faculties to a high degree of life; the other contracts, freezes and nearly annihilates them. I apprehend, that neither Shakespeare nor Milton by their fictions, nor Mr. Burke by his reasoning, anywhere looked to positive horror as a source of the sublime, though they all agree that terror is a very high one.

There were authors at the time with a different agenda. Matthew Lewis's *The Monk* (1796) lies more firmly in the "horror" side of gothic literature, featuring graphic scenes of rape, murder, and incest.

Samuel Taylor Coleridge, who embraced the gothic aesthetic in his "mystery poems," including "The Rime of the Ancient Mariner" and "Christabel," declared, "Situations of torment, and images of naked horror, are easily conceived; and a writer in whose works they abound, deserves our gratitude almost equally with him who should drag us by way of sport through a military hospital, or force us to sit at the dissecting-table of a natural philosopher." Yikes.

Moral Exchange

John Keats admired the effect of gothic literature, incorporating elements in poems such as "La Belle Dame sans Merci," with its mysterious gothic ladies, and "The Eve of St. Agnes," despite his teasing comment to a friend that, "I intend to tip you the Damosel Radcliffe—I'll cavern you, and grotto you, and waterfall you, and wood you, and water you, and immense-rock you, and tremendous sound you, and solitude you."

$2.50

THE DELUGE AT NORDERNEY—Of a maid, her lover, a Cardinal who was too good an actor, and a lady who was a little mad. And of how they faced death together, each in his own fashion, when the waters rose.

THE OLD CHEVALIER—Of what befell when Baron von Brackel took to his room a lovely stranger. And of the female skull which, fifteen years later, an artist prized as a precious work of art.

THE MONKEY—Of an exquisite but perverse young officer of the Royal Guards, of the Prioress's desire that he marry, of a maiden's strange visit to a convent, and of the part a monkey played.

THE ROADS ROUND PISA—Of Prince Nino of Tuscany, who kept the old ways of his land, and of how an old nobleman cheated death at his hands.

THE SUPPER AT ELSINORE—Of two great ladies of Denmark, and of the curious tryst they kept with their pirate brother, long since dead, whose ship had been his love.

THE DREAMERS—Of a beautiful Italian singer and of her strange shadow, told in the manner of the Arabian Nights.

THE POET—Of how a girl came to murder an old man, already wounded by her lover, because he longed to create a great poem.

These stories (or novelettes, rather, for they average twenty thousand words) are unique; we know of nothing quite like them in the English language. This statement will have to be taken largely on faith, for obviously our brief summaries cannot possibly do justice to the book's qualities. And

(See back flap)

[Jacket by F. J. Buttera]

Seven Gothic Tales

Isak Dinesen

Introduction by Dorothy Canfield

HARRISON SMITH ROBERT HAAS

Shakes Does It Again

In "On the Supernatural," Radcliffe credits Shakespeare with some of the scariest scenes in literature. She writes that the first appearance of the ghost of Hamlet's father is "above every ideal," and that, "Every minute circumstance of the scene between those watching on the platform, and of that between them and Horatio . . . [leads] on toward that high curiosity and thrilling awe with which we witness the conclusion of the scene."

Perhaps the most iconic moment of ghost-storytelling in the history of literature took place when a group of Romantic writers gathered in the summer of 1816 at the Villa Diodati in Switzerland. Mary Shelley, Percy Shelley, and John Polidori sat with Lord Byron, who had rented the villa for the summer. While it may have been the middle of June, the year 1816 was actually considered the "Year Without a Summer" due to its abnormal climate, which kept the writers inside as massive storms and flooding assaulted the continent.

In this appropriately gothic atmosphere, the four challenged each other to write their most frightening stories. The storytelling sprouted what would become Polidori's *The Vampyre,* which transformed the vampire of folklore into the modern aristocratic monster we think of today and spawned a whole subgenre of vampiric fiction; as well as, of course, Mary Shelley's *Frankenstein.* It's hard to find a more perfect embodiment of terror's creative power over the Romantics.

Gothic's popularity dissipated as the historical novels of Sir Walter Scott became the standard for the reading public, and the genre became more of a source of amusement for readers, particularly after Jane Austen's mock-gothic *Northanger Abbey* (1817). The novel about a seventeen-year-old girl with a love of gothic fiction and the frightful images she invents indicated the level of saturation gothic had reached at the time, yet it is more widely read today than the works she was mocking.

Did You Know?

Among the gothic novels discussed in *Northanger Abbey* are *The Castle of Wolfenbach, Mysterious Warnings, Necromancer of the Black Forest,* and *Horrid Mysteries.* Though it was assumed these were satiric titles invented by Austen, researchers recently discovered they are in fact early gothic works. Valancourt Books has since reprinted them in all their lurid detail.

Scary stories shifted in style during the Victorian age, with authors incorporating gothic elements into a range of different works. Dickens played with ghosts and ideas of moral retribution in *A Christmas Carol* (1843), and Charlotte Brontë incorporated the "madwoman in the attic" into *Jane Eyre* (1847). Henry James, Wilkie Collins, and Elizabeth Gaskell each incorporated elements of the supernatural and gothic into their works, while Edgar Allan Poe created his own brand of macabre.

Fear continued to be a valuable tool for writers late in the century as they used supernatural elements to explore ideas about burgeoning scientific discoveries as well as moral corruption. Works like Robert Louis Stevenson's *The Strange Case of Dr. Jekyll and Mr. Hyde* (1886), Oscar Wilde's *The Picture of Dorian Gray* (1890), and H. G. Wells's *The Island of Dr. Moreau* (1896) tapped into a fear that was based not on the past, with its ancient castles and mysteries, but on the frightening possibilities of the future.

Did You Know?

One of the final classic gothic novels is C. R. Maturin's *Melmoth the Wanderer* (1820), about a man who sells his soul for prolonged life. Following his trial, Oscar Wilde adopted the name Sebastian Melmoth in honor of Maturin's title character, but perhaps also a tip of his hat to the author, who happened to be his great uncle.

The Southern gothic tradition of the mid-twentieth century further updated the genre by transplanting gothic archetypes into the modern world of the American South. Flannery O'Connor, William Faulkner, and Carson McCullers, among others, used grotesque characters and an ominous sense of terror to provide a backdrop for their investigations of morality and decay.

With the continuing demand for spine-tingling tales, both at the bookstore and in the movie theater, optimism about the future of fear in literature seems justified.

WHY DO SOME DETECTIVES USE THEIR MINDS AND OTHERS THEIR FISTS?

The crime-solving skills of Holmes, Marlowe, and more

Crime solvers come in all shapes and sizes, from elderly spinsters to hardened private eyes, which may explain why detective stories continue to be devoured by readers regardless of age and taste. Any detective worth his or her salt gets the bad guy, but they have used drastically different tactics to do so, from keen observation to morally questionable trickery or brute force.

Edgar Allan Poe created the first literary detective, C. Auguste Dupin, in his 1841 story "The Murders in the Rue Morgue." Dupin is an intellectual and an avid reader who spots significance in minute details. He uses what he calls "ratiocination" to follow the criminal's thought process and seemingly read minds, all while dazzling his friend (the narrator of the story), and showing up the bumbling police force.

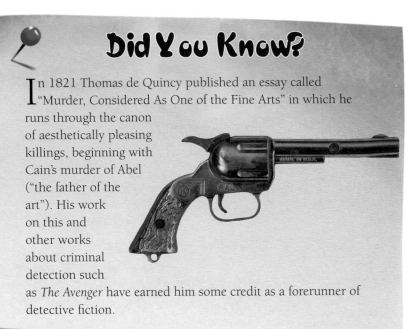

Did You Know?

In 1821 Thomas de Quincy published an essay called "Murder, Considered As One of the Fine Arts" in which he runs through the canon of aesthetically pleasing killings, beginning with Cain's murder of Abel ("the father of the art"). His work on this and other works about criminal detection such as *The Avenger* have earned him some credit as a forerunner of detective fiction.

Sound familiar?

Sir Arthur Conan Doyle acknowledges the influence of Poe in the first story featuring the character who would quickly become the most famous detective of all time. In *A Study in Scarlet*, Doctor Watson compares his friend Sherlock Holmes to Dupin, to which the less-than-humble Holmes replies, "No doubt you think you are complimenting me . . . In my opinion, Dupin was a very inferior fellow."

While Holmes is best known for his intellect, Conan Doyle made it clear that he was no brainy weakling. In *The Sign of Four*, the detective describes his early skill in bare-knuckle fighting, and the story *The Adventure of the Gloria Scott* mentions that he was trained as a boxer. Holmes goes mano a mano with opponents several times, explaining to Doctor Watson that he escaped Professor Moriarty by using *baritsu*, a Japanese system of martial arts.

Did You Know?

Arthur Conan Doyle's father did the original drawings for *A Study in Scarlet*, but they portrayed Sherlock Holmes as portly and squat, an odd interpretation of the character his son described. For the later pieces published in *The Stand* magazine, Sidney Paget was brought in to illustrate, making Holmes the slim dandy readers have come to love.

Holmes had other precursors and contemporaries, almost all British, including Charles Dickens's Inspector Bucket in *Bleak House* (1853), the first detective to appear in an English novel, and Wilkie Collins's Sergeant Cuff, reputedly the finest detective in England, in *The Moonstone* (1868).

Father Brown, who appears in more than fifty of G. K. Chesterton's short stories, was inspired by Holmes, but is a much different sort than the detective. Short and stout, he uses intuition to put himself in the mind of the killer, rather than deduction, and is a deeply religious man who uses his knowledge of men's sins to help him understand the criminals he pursues.

Together, these varied characters helped to usher in what is considered the "Golden Age of Detective Fiction," between 1920 and 1940, when the novel grew to be the prominent form of the detective story under the pens of Agatha Christie, Dorothy Sayers, and Margery Allingham (women writers dominated the genre throughout this period). As with the earlier stories, these followed the basic structure of tightly formed tales, taking place in a country house or some other isolated location, where a body is found, an assortment of red herrings are presented, and the story wraps up with the detective dramatically revealing the killer.

The Original Sleuth

It has been argued that the first detective we find in fiction is Oedipus. Like many of the great detective stories, the play begins with a crime as the King is murdered and Oedipus must find the killer through interrogating witnesses and deciphering clues. Of course, finding himself guilty of the crime likely presented problems for having Oedipus return in later episodes.

Detective fiction became, much like the crossword puzzles that were exploding in popularity around the same time, a sort of parlor game for the British audience still recovering from World War I. The aristocratic social values of the characters are threatened by the evil deeds of the killer, but order is soon restored through the reason and the cleverness of the detective. As the investigator outs the murderer, he (or occasionally she) also exonerates the rest of the characters, allowing life to smoothly resume as it was.

As the keepers of order, the detectives are dignified and disciplined themselves, like the impeccably neat Hercule Poirot of Christie's hugely popular whodunnits, or Sayers's aristocratic sleuth Lord Peter Wimsey. The narratives also had a clear, predictable structure, perhaps best laid out by crime writer Ronald Knox's "Ten Commandments" for detective stories:

1. The criminal must be mentioned in the early part of the story, but must not be anyone whose thoughts the reader has been allowed to know.
2. All supernatural or preternatural agencies are ruled out as a matter of course.
3. Not more than one secret room or passage is allowable.
4. No hitherto undiscovered poisons may be used, nor any appliance which will need a long scientific explanation at the end.
5. No Chinaman must figure in the story.
6. No accident must ever help the detective, nor must he ever have an unaccountable intuition which proves to be right.
7. The detective himself must not commit the crime.
8. The detective is bound to declare any clues which he may discover.
9. The stupid friend of the detective, the Watson, must not conceal from the reader any thoughts which pass through his mind: his intelligence must be slightly, but very slightly, below that of the average reader.

10. Twin brothers, and doubles generally, must not appear unless we have been duly prepared for them.

A Life of Their Own

On occasion, crime writers have found themselves at the mercy of their own creations. Arthur Conan Doyle famously tried to kill off Sherlock Holmes so he could move on to more serious writing, only to bring him back after immense public pressure, including accusations of having "murdered" the detective.

Agatha Christie described the portly Belgian Hercule Poirot to be a "detestable, bombastic, tiresome, ego-centric little creep," but could not bring herself to kill him off, saying, "he has to go on because people ask for him so much."

Leave it to Americans to throw all this out the window. While a fairly conservative approach to solving crime was selling massive quantities of mystery novels in Britain, American writers like Raymond Chandler, James M. Cain, and Dashiell Hammett turned mysteries into something decidedly darker.

Evolving from pulp magazines such as *Black Mask* which had grown in popularity after World War I, these "hard-boiled" stories gave us detectives, like Hammett's Sam Spade and Chandler's Philip Marlowe, who live in a stark and violent world. They do not see a clear line between criminals and the law, often engaging in illegal acts themselves in the process of solving crimes.

Hardly the model of genteel reserve, these tough guys were usually on the verge of going broke, and their diets generally

Did You Know?

Dashiell Hammett actually worked for several years as a detective for the Pinkerton agency, experiences that would later influence his novels, including *The Maltese Falcon* (1930) and *The Thin Man* (1934). He may have been too good—legend has it that in one case a man he was tailing got lost and Hammett had to offer him directions back to the city.

consisted of a combination of coffee and cigarettes. They often came to blows with adversaries, but without any talk of professional training. The narrative is similarly shadowy, with cases that begin seeming to be straightforward, but spiral into complicated mazes of strange characters and situations.

The hard-boiled camp of crime solving is particularly American in its embrace of the macho rebel who flouts convention and is less interested in maintaining social order than getting paid for his time. The works can also be seen as a return to Poe's original approach to detective fiction, with its gritty urban environments and focus on the city's underbelly.

When a reporter asked T. S. Eliot what he was receiving the Nobel Prize for, Eliot replied that it was for "the entire corpus" of his work. The confused reporter asked, "And when did you publish that?" Eliot said later that *The Entire Corpus* would make a good title for a mystery.

In recent decades the hard-boiled detectives have cleaned themselves up a little, as "police procedurals" have become the dominant type of detective story. These works, whether in novels like *Last Seen Wearing . . .* (1952) and the later novels of Dennis Lehane and Richard Price (as well as prime-time television shows from *Dragnet* to *Law & Order*) look at the details of official investigative techniques, including interrogations, forensics, autopsies, and even paperwork. The heroes are less likely to find themselves in harm's way, but the works remain much grittier than anything Agatha Christie would write.

Perhaps the most significant trend in detective stories since the end of World War II is that they are often not "detective stories" at all. Instead, writers in the genre are more likely to offer "crime novels," where character is more significant than plot, often with the reader already knowing who is the killer at the beginning of the story. From true-crime pulps to Thomas Harris's Hannibal Lecter novels to "nonfiction novels" including Truman Capote's

In Cold Blood (1965), the killer plays a more prominent role than the detective.

With works like Dan Brown's *The Da Vinci Code* and Stieg Larsson's *Millennium* trilogy dominating bestseller lists, it seems, at least for now, that the detectives are still one step ahead of the criminals.

Be Careful What Company You Keep

Norman Mailer pushed for the publication of convict Jack Henry Abbott's *In the Belly of the Beast* and then helped to secure his release from prison, only to have Abbot murder a man six weeks later—the day before *The New York Times* published a rave review of his book. Mailer may have been tough, but his power of observation would have needed some work if he ever wanted to be a detective.

WHAT OTHER UNCONTROLLABLE MONSTER DID DR. FRANKENSTEIN INVENT?

The birth and spread of science fiction

Victor Frankenstein describes the moment when, "the dull yellow eye of the creature open[ed]; it breathed hard, and a convulsive motion agitated its limbs." Of course, these lines from Mary Shelley's *Frankenstein* refer to the frightful, unnamed creature the doctor has cobbled together with parts from collected bones and discarded parts. This moment is also when the first spark of life appeared in a nascent literary genre that would develop into an amalgam of romance, horror, and scientific inquiry that its creator could hardly have predicted at the time: science fiction.

Shelley's work, with a monster devised through scientific research and technical skill, presents science as a source of transcendence at once inspiring and terrifying and set in motion a new way for writers to examine their rapidly changing world.

Early works by Poe, such as *The Unparalleled Adventures of One Hans Pfaall* (1850), as well as others flitting between journalism and tall tales, set the stage for Jules Verne and H. G. Wells, who would popularize the genre later in the century. After reading Poe in 1856, Jules and Edmond de Goncourt described his work in their *Journal des Goncourt* as "a new literary world pointing to the literature of the twentieth century. Scientific miracles, fables on the pattern A + B; a clear-sighted, sickly literature. No more poetry, but analytic fantasy." They would prove to be right on the mark.

Verne, a student of geology, paleontology, and evolutionary biology, wrote works that combined his interests with an adventurous and pioneering spirit. Just as the attention to scientific detail gave the works of Shelley and Poe an element of realism, Verne instilled his novels with at least partly plausible science. Works like *A Journey to the Centre of the Earth* (1864), *From the Earth to the Moon* (1865), *Twenty Thousand Leagues Under the Sea*

(1869–1870), *Around the World in Eighty Days* (1873), and *The Mysterious Island* (1875) expanded the audience for the growing genre.

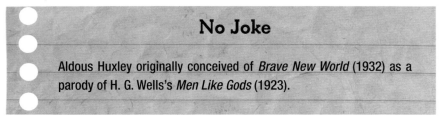

No Joke

Aldous Huxley originally conceived of *Brave New World* (1932) as a parody of H. G. Wells's *Men Like Gods* (1923).

Wells described his works, such as *The Time Machine* (1895) and *The War of the Worlds* (1898), as "scientific romances," reflecting the connection they had to Mary Shelley's gothic tradition. Incorporating notions of alien planets, new technology, and the possibilities of human invention, his themes would be fundamental to later works in the genre.

"Scientific romance" became "science fiction" in 1926. The man who rechristened it, Hugo Gernsback, was publisher of *Amazing Stories*, the first of what would be many pulp magazines dedicated to the genre, including *Science Wonder Stories* and *Astounding Science Fiction*. For decades, these magazines became the primary outlet for both upcoming and established science fiction authors.

www.shutterstock.com · 30600223

Did You Know?

Gernsback was not particularly generous in paying his writers and a bit shady in his running of the magazine—which is why H. P. Lovecraft dubbed him "Hugo the Rat." Nonetheless, he would become the namesake for one of science fiction's most respected awards, the "Hugos."

Although many of these early stories were exuberant works of adventure set on other planets, sometimes derisively referred to as "space operas," by the mid-1930s, the anxiety of the Depression and World War II had imparted a more sober approach to the style. The dystopian novels of George Orwell's *Nineteen Eighty-Four* (1949) and Aldous Huxley's *Ape and Essence* (1949) were produced outside the science fiction community, but their tone and themes would prove an influence on later works.

For readers outside the genre, this culture of pulp magazines stuffed with stories of varying quality seemed quite foreign. During the late 1950s, two prominent authors helped translate this strange world for a more mainstream audience:

- In a 1955 talk to Cambridge University, C. S. Lewis commented on the improving quality of the genre, saying that fifteen years before it was "usually detestable; the conceptions, sometimes worthy of better treatments." But that more recently, "there was an improvement: not that very bad stories cease to be the majority, but that the good ones became better and more numerous."
- Four years later, Kingsley Amis published the ingeniously titled *New Maps of Hell*, in which he provides a brief history of the genre, offering, "to read, and to study, science fiction are valid and interesting pursuits from any old point of view, whether literary, sociological, psychological, political, or what you will, though the first of these will probably keep you going longer than any of the others."

The rise of science fiction's "Big Three"—Arthur C. Clarke, Robert Heinlein, and Isaac Asimov—firmly established the genre for the twentieth century. Each one made major contributions with crossover appeal to the uninitiated, from Asimov's 1941 short story "Nightfall" (anthologized some four dozen times), and Heinlein's politically charged *Starship Troopers* (1959) to Clarke's novel *Childhood's End* (1953), about the further evolution of the human race, as well as dozens of other works.

Life Imitates Art

Science fiction has also had a history of helping spark innovation and inspiring actual scientists in their efforts. H. G. Wells correctly predicted the invention of wheeled trucks, air conditioning, video recording, propeller airplanes, and television.

Arthur C. Clarke predicted that "personal radios" would be invented in 1980–1990 (a fairly accurate prediction of the Walkman), and that a "global library" would be in existence by the year 2005—not far off from the growth of the Internet.

With the publication of *The Left Hand of Darkness* (1969) and *The Dispossessed* (1974), Ursula K. Le Guin established herself as the most significant female voice in the genre since Mary Shelley. Her works use tales of alien cultures to examine human society and explore ideas of sexual identity, earning her interest from feminists.

John Wyndham, Brian Aldiss, J. G. Ballard, and John Brunner, incorporated a more playful tone into the anxious concerns about science. As the use of computers grew, William Gibson and his fellow cyberpunk writers ushered in an era of dark dystopian visions, which helped to reenergize the genre. Gibson coined the term "cyberspace" in his *Neuromancer* (1984). Far from the optimistic "romances," cyberpunk novels brought a noir pessimism to their accounts of hackers fighting a dismal future.

Did You Know?

The broad appeal of science fiction is apparent in the many writers outside the genre who have used its elements in their writing. Among them are Kurt Vonnegut in *Cat's Cradle* (1963), Doris Lessing in her space fiction series *Canopus in Argos: Archives* (1979–1983), Thomas Pynchon in *Gravity's Rainbow* (1973), and Gore Vidal's *Kalki* (1978).

Some of the genre's biggest contributions to popular culture have been through film adaptations. Just as Boris Karloff as Frankenstein's monster is one of the first images to come to mind when we hear "Frankenstein," the works of science fiction writers are constantly adapted into major films, from Philip K. Dick's novel *Do Androids Dream of Electric Sheep?* (1968) serving as the basis for the blockbuster *Blade Runner* (1982) to Clarke's collaboration with director Stanley Kubrick on the critically acclaimed *2001: A Space Odyssey* (1968) to the more recent *I Am Legend* (2007), based on Richard Matheson's 1954 novel. While many of these take liberties with their source material, and only occasionally involve the authors creatively in the adaptations, mainstream audiences often first connect with the genre through the big screen.

Like Frankenstein's monster, science fiction remains something of an outsider to the broader literary world. Rather than worrying about what the Pulitzer committee thinks of the work of the genre's masters, the science fiction community has developed its own extensive award system. Besides the Science Fiction and Fantasy Hall of Fame in Seattle, Washington, there are also the Hugo Awards, Nebula Awards, John W. Campbell Awards, and Philip K. Dick Awards.

This might help explain why the genre continues to have one of the most passionate and loyal fan bases. Groups such as San Diego–based Darkstar, the male-only Trap Door Spiders (whose members included Isaac Asimov), and Broad Universe (which promotes works by women science fiction writers) cater to the genre's enthusiastic writers and followers, providing online platforms, conventions, and events where they can meet and discuss their favorite works. Science fiction writer Cory Doctorow calls the genre "perhaps the most social of all literary genres." While the genre may still reside a bit outside the literary mainstream, this is far from a lonely place.

CONCLUSION: LAST WORDS

We'll wrap up this volume with a few ways that writers have wrapped up their lives. Though literature's greats could not choose when they went, many found ways to exit poetically:

Making arrangements for his own funeral, Hans Christian Andersen instructed the musician, "Most of the people who will walk after me will be children, so make the beat keep time with little steps."

Molière was struck down by tuberculosis while performing his play *The Imaginary Invalid.* His hacking cough led to a collapse, and he was rushed to the hospital, but it was too late. Ironically he was playing the role of the hypochondriac in the play.

Thomas More (1516), author of *Utopia,* was imprisoned and executed for treason. His final words to his executioner: "Pluck up thy spirits, man, and be not afraid to do thine office. My neck is very short, take heed therefore thou strike not awry for saving thine honesty."

Ben Jonson is the only person to be buried sitting in an upright position in Westmister Abbey. He asked his benefactor, Charles I of England, to give him only a square foot in the hallowed cemetery.

Famous Last Words:

Johann Goethe:	"Open the second shutter so that more light may come in."
O. Henry:	"Don't turn down the light. I'm afraid to go home in the dark."
James Joyce:	"Does nobody understand?"
Washington Irving:	"I must arrange my pillows for another night. When will this end?"
Henry James:	"So it has come at last—the Distin-guished Thing."

Benjamin Franklin composed his own epitaph:

> The body of B. Franklin, printer,
> Like the cover of an old book,
> Its contents torn out,
> And stript of its lettering and gilding
> Lies here, food for worms.
> But the work itself shall not be lost;
> For it will, as he believed, appear once more
> In a new and more elegant edition,
> Corrected and amended
> By its author.

SELECTED BIBLIOGRAPHY

B esides all the great novels, poems, and tales referred to in this work, these are the main works that supplied me with facts and anecdotes, and contributed to my thinking:

Bartlett's Book of Anecdotes. Edited by Clifton Fadiman and Andre Bernard (New York: Little, Brown, revised 2000).

Bloom, Clive. *Bestsellers: Popular Fiction Since 1900* (Hampshire, UK: Palgrave Macmillan, 2003).

Boon, Marcus. *The Road of Excess: A History of Writers on Drugs* (Boston: Harvard University Press, 2002).

Brantlinger, Patrick. *The Reading Lesson: The Threat of Mass Literacy in Nineteenth-century British Fiction* (Bloomington: Indiana University Press, 1998).

Burt, Daniel S. *The Literary 100: A Ranking of the Most Influential Novelists, Playwrights, and Poets of All Time* (New York: Checkmark Books, 2001).

Cox, John D. *The Devil and the Sacred in English Drama, 1350–1642* (New York: Cambridge University Press, 2000).

Demers, Patricia. *From Instruction to Delight: An Anthology of Children's Literature to 1850* (New York: Oxford University Press, 2003).

Eisner, Eric. *Nineteenth Century Poetry and Literary Celebrity* (Hampshire, UK: Palgrave Macmillan, 2009).

Gilbar, Steven. *Bibliotopia, or, Mr. Gilbar's Book of Books & Catch-all of Literary Facts and Curiosities* (Boston: David R Godine, 2005).

Glass, Loren Daniel. *Authors Inc.: Literary Celebrity in the Modern United States, 1880–1980* (New York: NYU Press, 2004).

Jackson, Mary V. *Engines of Instruction, Mischief, and Magic: Children's Literature in England from Its Beginnings to 1839* (Lincoln, NE: University of Nebraska Press, 1990).

Joshi, S. T. *Junk Fiction: America's Obsessions with Bestsellers* (Rockville, MD: Borgo Press, 2009).

Katsoulis, Melissa. *Literary Hoaxes: An Eye-Opening History of Famous Frauds* (New York: Skyhorse Publishing, 2009).

Kiernan, Pauline. *Filthy Shakespeare: Shakespeare's Most Outrageous Sexual Puns* (London: Quercus Publishing, 2006).

Lerer, Seth. *Children's Literature: A Reader's History from Aesop to Harry Potter* (Chicago: University of Chicago Press, 2008).

Lutz, Deborah. *The Dangerous Lover: Gothic Villains, Byronism, and the Nineteenth-Century Seductive Narrative* (Columbus: Ohio State University Press, 2006).

McDayter, Ghislaine. *Byromania and the Birth of Celebrity Culture* (Albany: State University of New York Press, 2009).

Moran, Joe. *Star Authors: Literary Celebrity in America* (London: Pluto Press, 2000).

The Norton Anthology of English Literature, Seventh Edition. Edited by M. H. Abrams and Stephen Greenblatt (New York: W. W. Norton, 2000).

Plant, Sadie. *Writing on Drugs* (New York: Farrar, Straus, and Giroux, 2000).

Schatz, Thomas. *The Genius of the System: Hollywood Filmmaking in the Studio Era* (New York: Holt Paperbacks, 1996).

Shannonhouse, Rebecca. *Under the Influence: The Literature of Addiction* (New York: Modern Library, 2003).

Vincent, David. *The Rise of Mass Literacy: Reading and Writing in Modern Europe* (New York: Polity, 2000).

Yagoda, Ben. *Memoir, A History* (New York: Riverhead Books, 2009).